GET OFF YOUR

ASH

GET OFF YOUR ASH

Backwards is the New Forward

JOE AMARAL

joeamaral

ONTARIO, CANADA

Cover artwork: Todd Stahl
Cover and book design and layout: Karen Amaral

Address: Box 245 • Milton, Ontario • L9T 1P0 • Canada

Website for this Book: getoffyourash.today
Author's Website: joeamaral.org

Author's Social Media links:
Facebook @joeamaralpublic
Instagram @joeamaral
Twitter @joeamaraltweet
Youtube @joeamaral

Podcast links:
Anchor https://anchor.fm/getoffyourash
Apple https://podcasts.apple.com/us/podcast/get-off-your-ash/id1592394240
Spotify https://open.spotify.com/show/0SYLFxUz6u1iTO7AaS0jaH

Printed in Canada: APD Printing • Brantford, ON

Dedication

This book is dedicated to anyone who has ever been made to feel less-than, unworthy or unable. You are so much more than your past has tried to make you out to be.

To all the people in my life who stood with me through the darkest of times. I could not have done it without your love and support. Your friendships have meant more to me than you will ever know.

Contents

GET OFF YOUR
ASH

Chapter 1
PAIN IN THE ASH

◇◇◇◇◇◇◇

And he took a piece of broken pottery with which to scrape himself while he sat in the ashes.
—Job 2:8

◇◇◇◇◇◇◇

OK. Let's talk about the elephant in the room. The book title, "Get Off Your Ash". What is it and what does it mean? Trust me, it's more than just a cheeky title or a clever play on words. There is actually a lot of beautiful and deep meaning behind it. Many of you are reading this book because you've been familiar with my work since 2002. To you folks, you already know my sense of humour. If you're new to the "Joe Amaral" thing, you should probably know that I consider myself somewhat of a funny man, and someone who is not afraid to push the envelope if it means that it will help get the message across and help people understand the point of the teaching. Anyway, let's get back to Job.

The title of the book is rooted in the Biblical story of Job. Even if you don't come from an overly religious background, you've probably heard his story. You may have even heard the stories but didn't know it was speaking of an actual man who lived more than 6000 years ago. His story is spectacular. It plays out like a blockbuster movie.

Job came from an area in the Middle East that has been commonly connected to either modern-day Jordan or Saudi Arabia. The Bible refers to it as the land of Uz. Job is described as a righteous man. He's a good dude, in a bad world. And then, out of nowhere, he starts to receive back-to-back messages about his possessions and his family that you never hope to hear in your lifetime.

The Biblical text goes as far as to say that no one was wealthier than Job in all the Lands of the East. He may not have been rich in the same sense as we would describe it. He didn't have a big house or a huge social media following. He was rich in the way people calculated wealth during that time. One word. Livestock. And lots of it. At the beginning of the book of Job, the text says he had 7000 sheep, 3000 camels, 500 yoke of oxen, 500 female donkeys. In your mind, imagine these livestock as having the same value as such modern-day items like televisions, sports cars, summer houses and the like. What do you think of Job now? Not too shabby, right?

I don't know if I can adequately describe how horrific the information was that Job was receiving. One moment, he was the king of his world. The next moment, he had lost everyone he had ever loved and everything he had ever worked hard for. We're told that as his children were eating and drinking together—having a party—a messenger came to Job and told him that every single one of his oxen and donkeys were killed with the sword by an invading army. Oxen and donkeys were used to plow the fields and carry equipment across vast distances. In total, he lost 1500 work animals. In today's vernacular, that would be like losing 1500 trucks and tractors. That, in and of itself, would be a disaster and a huge blow to your way of living. But it gets worse…much worse.

While this first messenger is still speaking—while he is still delivering the first bit of devastating news—a second messenger arrives. This time, the stakes are raised, Now Job is told that all 7000 of his sheep were killed in a fire, and that it was an act of God. You need to remember that the sheep was the product he would sell and trade. That would be like an Amazon warehouse burning to the ground with all of the inventory destroyed by fire. That would be an absolute calamity and it would more than likely tank that entire division. But again…it gets worse…

While the second messenger is speaking, a third messenger appears and tells Job that all 3000 of his camels were slaughtered! These animals were used to carry goods across the desert into foreign lands. They were Job's primary mode of transportation for what we would refer to as international trade. And just like that, they're gone. Every single last one of them. That would be like FedEx or Purolator having every single one of their planes destroyed. It would cripple the company and the loss of income would be incalculable. And then the final blow comes, the worst news any parent, anytime, anywhere, could ever receive. You guessed it—a fourth messenger appears as the third messenger is finishing.

Remember how all his children were all together in one place eating and drinking, having a party?

This fourth messenger bring news that would be the final straw in Job's pain and suffering. Job is told that a strong wind came and struck the house where all his children were. The house collapsed and killed all seven sons and all three daughters.

Just like that, in the blink of an eye, Job's entire life—all of his success, everything that he had sacrificed so much for—was gone. No business, no family, no legacy. Gone. Completely ravished and taken away. And all of it happens almost all at the same exact moment. I don't know that any one of us could identify with that level of loss, with that level of pain and heartbreak—that level of disappointment and brokenness. Add to this, as each messenger delivered their message of loss, every single servant who was working in their respective field was also killed. That means that Job's entire workforce was also wiped out. No equipment. No product. No staff. No transportation. No family. No hope.

How would you react? I have to be honest. Job's initial reaction was a bit surprising, but not unusual. I'll explain that in a minute. Look at what the text tells us in Job 1:20-21— "Then Job arose and tore his robe and shaved his head and fell on the ground and worshiped. And he said, 'Naked I came from my mother's womb, and naked shall I return. The LORD gave, and the LORD has taken away; blessed be the name of the LORD'." His initial response is a calm one. Kind of like an "oh well" type of reaction. I said that his response was not unusual. What did I mean by that?

Let me give you an example from my own life and see if you have ever had something similar happen to you. On October 22, 2008, my father died. He died of a Stage IV Glioblastoma Multiforme brain tumor. It was a brutal process. I watched a funny, vibrant, full-of-life man, be reduced to a paralyzed, eventually comatose, shadow of himself. The cancer ravaged his body, killing him slowly, methodically. It was truly sinister.

I was by his side when he took his last breath. Like Job, the moment it happened, I was ok with it. To be honest, I was actually relieved for my dad. His suffering had ended. He had finally been freed from the prison that his cancer caused his own body to become. But, like Job, that moment of passive delight would eventually fade and turn to the worst anger, hurt, pain and anguish that I had ever felt in my life. I shudder as I reflect on those moments.

The entire premise of this book, and from whence it gets its title, is from the following passage: Job 2:8— "And he took a piece of broken pottery with which to scrape himself while he sat in the ashes."

Job sat in ashes.

Sitting in ash or covering oneself in ash was a common custom during the time of Job. The use of ash in identifying with grief and pain was widespread. We know that it was used by many cultures around the world. But what is ash and what does it represent? I could bore you with a detailed analysis of what elements are present in ash, but I don't think either one of us would enjoy that. So, here's the "Ash For Dummies" version… "the powdery residue left after the burning of a substance." A simple Google search will generate a smattering in variation, but ash is simply all that remains once something is completely burnt.

Because ash represented the complete destruction and annihilation of what was burned, it became the universal sign for signalling that you were grieving. In other words, something in your life had recently been completely and utterly taken away and destroyed. Namely, a loved one. Losing your business or job is one thing. Losing your property is another thing. Losing all your children in one tragic accident is an entirely different thing. Job lost everything all at once. It was as if a symphony of tragedy was being recited to Job. So, although his initial reaction was one of acceptance and gentleness, that would quickly change. And it did.

We're told that Job sat in the ashes. But it wasn't just some random pile of ash. He didn't order it from somewhere or ask for it to be collected and brought to him. No, these were his ashes. We're not told how he got them. We're just told that he had enough ash to make a big enough pile that a grown man could sit on. So, where did he get all that ash from? I have a thought.

In Job 1:16 we're told that the sheep and servants were completely destroyed and wiped out by fire. It was common practice in those days to get rid of the dead, both human and animal, by burning the remains. Rotting animals and human corpses would produce an unimaginable stench in the hot middle eastern desert. So, burning was the method of choice. Given the fact that there were thousands of animal carcasses, burial seems unlikely. As for his heritage, some scholars believe he was of Hebrew descent, others say he was from Edom—that is, a Gentile. So, the burning of corpses would have been familiar to Job and his people at the time.

Here's my thought…just imagine for a second if you can. If Job gathered all the ashes of all that he had lost in one place—the ashes of the animals, the servants, and…his children—and made a pile big enough to sit on and mourn...Whoa! That's a powerful image to consider.

Gruesome, but not completely implausible. After all, don't people today keep the ashes of their loved ones in their homes? The ashes serve as a reminder of what has been lost. The tragedy and pain of the loss is always in plain sight. I can't describe or explain why, but the same ashes that remind us of the pain and loss, can also bring us a sense of comfort by simply being close by. So, Job sat on his ash. This is important because it reinforces the idea of how painful the trauma was that Job went through.

If we can understand and grasp the depth behind the imagery of Job sitting on his ash, we can truly come to a better and more compassionate view of what he was going through and why he sat on his ash for the next 40 chapters in the book of Job. He could have gotten up at any time. All through the book—when his wife is speaking to him…when his friends are speaking to him…even when God is speaking to him. He sits. He sits on his ash. In order to comprehend why he sat on his ash, it's important for us to recognize what the ash pile was made of.

You've been reading for a while now. I want you to stop for a moment and look at the book cover. Not the title or subtitle, but the artwork of the pile of ash. Look closely. You'll see that the swirls and lines that make up the pile of ash, are actually words. Not random words, but carefully selected ones. Words to express what Job was going through. Words to express the thoughts and feelings that you and I go through. I wonder, if I was to ask you to share your journey, what words would make it to the cover of this book. Perhaps there would be words like "pain", "fear", "shame", "hurt", "guilt", etc…

Job wasn't just sitting on some metaphorical pile of ash; he was sitting on an actual pile of ash. There was meaning in that ash. It was personal for Job. He didn't know what to do and couldn't do anything about what had happened to him. He and his friends spent almost 40 chapters together trying to reason and understand the "why" of it all. Haven't we all done the very same thing? One of the elements of my own personal ash pile was my father's death. I must have asked God a thousand times, "Why?" Just like Job tried to figure out why God would allow such a horrible thing to happen to such a good guy. My dad was a good guy. Why him?

Job was literally sitting on his pain. That's why this chapter is called, "Pain in the Ash". Because it's true. Because we all have pain and trauma that we "sit" on. We stew in it. Sometimes for hours or days. Some sit for months and even for years. And still, some sit on their ash for decades. There's something oddly satisfying about pain. Although at times the pain is indescribably agonizing to bear and can tear us up inside, somehow, someway, being anchored to our pain provides comfort and connection to that which we once valued. In our own twisted sense of reasoning, sitting on our ash honors what we went through, and in the case of the loss of a loved one, it somehow keeps them alive, even if it's only manifested in our pain.

Sitting on our ash is a very dangerous thing to do indeed. The longer we sit, the more comfortable and familiar the pain becomes. Here's the sick and twisted danger that comes with sitting on your ash for too long: we get so used to it. It becomes a part of us. It feeds into our identity and our sense of being. The longer we sit on our ash, the more it enters into our being and becomes the essence of who we are. Ultimately, it can even alter our personality. When we live with the memory of pain, guilt or shame long enough, without even realizing it, we begin to modify our thoughts and eventually, it manifests itself in our actions.

The poison of sitting on your ash for too long is that it will seep into your system of thinking and behaving. Not only can it reshape your personality, it can also rob you of your passion. The longer we sit on our collective ashes, the more difficult it will become to separate who we really are from what we have become. Once the pain of your ash enters into your daily way of living and thinking, it becomes such a part of you, that you can't even remember what you were like before. Some people are scared to death of what they will become if they get off their ash and begin the healing process. I didn't read this stuff in a book. I didn't search for it online. I've lived it. In some ways, I'm still living it. And if I'm prepared to be fully honest with myself, and with you, a small part of me will always be living it.

Job sat on his ash. This Joe has been sitting on his ash too. All our ash piles may be made up of different elements and experiences, but in the end, they're just as real and powerful to whomever has lived that life and gone through that experience. For me personally, the pain in my ash was shame. Shame of what happened to me as a young boy. Shame of what would happen if people ever found out. What would people say? What would people think? These questions lived rent-free in my brain for many years. As a survivor of male, childhood sexual abuse, I fully understand the fear of letting go and moving on from the pain of the past.

2015.

The 2015 date above is not a type setting error, nor is it an oversight by my editing team. Not only is it its own paragraph, but it could be its own chapter…maybe even its own book. While the purpose of this book is not to fully explore the events of my sexual abuse, it is important to speak about the effects of that experience.

2015 was, without a doubt, the absolute worst year of my life as the memories of what had happened to me as a child began to resurface. While I was still a regular on Canadian television, travelling the world speaking at prestigious churches and events,

I was dying on the inside. I was dying mentally, emotionally, spiritually, as well as physically.

My body began manifesting the hurt that my mind had been hiding from me for more than 30 years. I had never heard the word "repressed" before. I'd heard of "suppressed" and "depressed", but "repressed" was a new one for me. It wasn't that I was trying to forget what happened to me, it's that my mind buried the memories so deep because they were too traumatic and painful for me to deal with. My body and my mind were not prepared to have that conversation. I became quite ill. I developed destructive habits and psychological disorders that I never dreamed I would have. I became prone to panic attacks. I developed a severe phobia of large crowds and noisy environments. I fell into depression and started to experience frequent bouts of anxiety.

The behavior that I was exhibiting was because I wasn't able to deal with the pain I had amassed over a lifetime. I call it "Trauma-Drama". To compensate, without being aware of it, the pain began to alter my personality. I had been subconsciously over-compensating with a big personality in order to cover up the pain and shame of the abuse. I was always the life of the party. I was the funny guy.

Without realizing it, I was keeping my brain busy by writing, speaking and travelling, just so my mind wouldn't find the time to deal with the ash. I wore the mask of confidence so well. But the truth is, there was a scared, neglected and hurt little boy still living on the inside. When it finally came time for me to get off my ash and deal with the pain, it meant ripping off the mask I had been wearing for the majority of my adult life. The mask had become such a part of who I was. And if I'm being completely honest, ripping it off was a torturous and tedious process, but it was the best thing I ever did.

We can't always control what happens to us. The actions taken against us are often out of our control. But what we can control, we should control. So, what can we control? Our reaction. And that's where things went off the rails for Job. As we already discussed, his initial reaction was one of acceptance and understanding, but after a while, acceptance turned into anger and understanding turned into unforgiveness. He had taken all that he could handle, and when it all became too much, he buckled under the pressure. He gathered up his ash and he sat. He stewed. He steamed. He sulked.

He went on one of the most epic rants ever recorded in history. I mean, the boy could complain! And complain he did! His spiel about the day of his birth has to go down as one of the most self-loathing pieces of literature in all of human history. It's absolutely stunning how much his perspective changed regarding his birth. He used to celebrate it with all of his children. That's what Job 1:4 says—"His sons used to go and hold a feast in the house of each one on his day, and they would send and invite their three sisters to eat and drink with them."

When life was good, so was his perspective. But as soon as things didn't go according to plan, he pulls a full 180° and goes in the complete and opposite direction. He devotes all of chapter three to how much he regrets the day of his birth. Twenty-six verses filled with nothing but regret and disdain for the day he was born. Don't believe me? Here it is in all of its glory.

> 1 After this Job opened his mouth and cursed
> the day of his birth. 2 And Job said:
> 3 "Let the day perish on which I was born,
> and the night that said, 'A man is conceived.'
> 4 Let that day be darkness! May God above
> not seek it, nor light shine upon it.

5 Let gloom and deep darkness claim it. Let clouds dwell upon it; let the blackness of the day terrify it.

6 That night—let thick darkness seize it! Let it not rejoice among the days of the year; let it not come into the number of the months.

7 Behold, let that night be barren; let no joyful cry enter it.

8 Let those curse it who curse the day, who are ready to rouse up Leviathan.

9 Let the stars of its dawn be dark; let it hope for light, but have none, nor see the eyelids of the morning,

10 because it did not shut the doors of my mother's womb, nor hide trouble from my eyes.

11 "Why did I not die at birth, come out from the womb and expire?

12 Why did the knees receive me? Or why the breasts, that I should nurse?

13 For then I would have lain down and been quiet; I would have slept; then I would have been at rest,

14 with kings and counselors of the earth who rebuilt ruins for themselves,

15 or with princes who had gold, who filled their houses with silver.

16 Or why was I not as a hidden stillborn child, as infants who never see the light?
17 There the wicked cease from troubling, and there the weary are at rest.
18 There the prisoners are at ease together; they hear not the voice of the taskmaster.
19 The small and the great are there, and the slave is free from his master.
20 "Why is light given to him who is in misery, and life to the bitter in soul,
21 who long for death, but it comes not, and dig for it more than for hidden treasures,
22 who rejoice exceedingly and are glad when they find the grave?
23 Why is light given to a man whose way is hidden, whom God has hedged in?
24 For my sighing comes instead of my bread, and my groanings are poured out like water.
25 For the thing that I fear comes upon me, and what I dread befalls me.
26 I am not at ease, nor am I quiet; I have no rest, but trouble comes."

Told you. Epic! Right? This is the problem of Job. He has the total freedom in how to respond to his situation. What does he do? He chooses to sit on his ash, his pain, his anger, his resentment. He chooses to be sad. He chooses to be mad.

Now, before you get all judgemental with Job, let's take a step back and a closer look at our own lives. How do you respond to something that happened to you that wasn't planned? What was your default posture when the proverbial rug was pulled out from under your feet? How did you behave when your world came crashing down? You may not have written twenty-six epic verses cursing the day of your birth, but I'd bet you experienced a few choice thoughts—maybe even a few choice words too.

You see, that's the thing about pain. In its own sick and twisted way, it unites us in a common human experience. I'm not saying that it is easy or even natural to react positively to a negative situation. But after taking a brief look at the life of Job, don't you think you owe it to yourself and those around you to choose differently? You're not alone in experiencing pain in the ash. We all go through it. The key is not that we all go through it but how we go through it. What happens through you is as powerful as what happens to you.

The life of Job shows us what can happen to a person when they sit on their ash and choose to remain living in the pain. We all know the cheesy adage, "Be better, not bitter". It's true though. Job got better towards the end of his life, but it took a long time to get there. He went to a dark place very quickly. The truth is that many of us have done, and continue doing, the same thing over and over again. It's easy to get down on yourself when things go wrong. It's understandable to punish yourself for someone else's actions.

One of the first things in our lives to be impacted by the pain in our ash, is our self-identity and self-confidence. When you feel broken, it's hard to fit into a society that glorifies perfection. It's hard for other people to see you as whole, as a person of value, when you can't even see it in yourself.

It's amazing and absolutely ludicrous that we are so quick to blame ourselves for other people's evil. It can cause self-doubt and in extreme cases, even self-hate. Have you ever experienced this? I know I have. There have been times that I have been so angry with myself. Not just because of something I thought, said or did, but because I've allowed my opinion of myself to be shaped by others.

Would it surprise you to find out that Job was having a tough time loving himself and his life? Well, it's true. He doesn't just say it once, but he actually says on three separate occasions in a short span of time. Not only does he admit to not liking himself, but he takes it two steps further. Doubting, or not liking yourself is one thing. Saying that you hate yourself or your life is a much more serious thing. But Job goes to the extreme and says that he actually loathes his life. You have to be in a pretty dark place in order to say that about yourself. To loathe something is to more than just hate it. It's to despise, abhor or detest something or someone. Just think of how low you have to be or how much pain you are feeling in order to say that you loathe something or someone.

Our family are big movie people. When our kids were younger, they would latch on to one particular film and watch it over, and over, and over, and over again! When they were little, I remember it being "George of the Jungle". They loved that movie. It would play at least twice a day, sometimes three! We eventually wore out the VHS tape. For those of you who are 30 or under, Google what a VHS player was. For a while it was the first "Shrek" movie. By then we had upgraded to DVD. If you are 20 or under, Google what a DVD player was! Then it was "The Lion King", and pretty much every Disney movie that came out in the early 2000's.

But the one movie that not only stands out the most, but the one that we quote from the most, the undisputed champion is…Ron Howard's 2000 release of "How the Grinch Stole Christmas", starring Canadian-born actor, Jim Carrey. I know it's supposed to be a Christmas movie, but we watched that thing all year round. It made us laugh then, and it still does now. Not only were we big movie watchers as a family, we also became big movie quoters. Are we the only ones, or does anyone else out there do this too? My dear son-in-law would laugh at us all the time. He just knew, that when a certain situation came up, we were going to quote a movie line. I think he's finally getting used to it.

The one from the Grinch isn't just funny, it oddly goes right along with what we were just saying about how Job loathed his life. Let me paint the picture for you. The Grinch is at his awesome lair, high in the clouds on top of Mount Crumpit. He has several bizarre and hilarious traditions. One of them, is to read through the names of the various people who live down in Whoville and express his absolute disdain for them. As he reads through the names, he says… "Hate, hate, hate, hate, hate, hate, double hate, *LOOOATHE ENTIRELY!*" OK. If you haven't ever seen this scene, first off, where have you been? Secondly, put the book down right now and search the above phrase on YouTube. Trust me, you'll thank me later.

It's a hilarious scene, but the director is really trying to get across how abandoned and lonely the Grinch feels. So much so, that it has caused him to utterly loathe someone. Think about how much you'd have to dislike someone in order to say that you loathe them. And yet, Job, not once, but three times, admits to loathing his life. One can only imagine the darkness he was facing as he repeatedly stated how awful his life was. Here are the three references:

Job 7:16a—I loathe my life.

Job 9:21—I loathe my life.

Job 10:1—I loathe my life.

Not only did sitting on his ash rob him of the joy of life, it also robbed him of his purpose and passion. We're going to explore this phenomenon in a later chapter. How can sitting on your ash actually alter your personality, steal your joy, and prevent you from pursuing your passion? Also, how did Job go from a man who sat on his ash and whined and complained about his situation?

...Who blamed everyone under the sun for his problems but himself? ...Go to being a man who was doubly blessed by God? As we continue to look at the life of Job, one thing jumps out. There came a place and time where he was willing to risk leaving behind the safety and comfort of his pain and exchange it for freedom. In short, Job got off his ash.

So, what's the pain in your ash that you are choosing to continually live with? And now that we've realized that we have been sitting on our ash, and admitted that we have become comfortable with the pain, what do we do now? Well...now it's time to move your ash! Are you ready? Let's go!

A personal note from me...please don't skip the worksheet at the end of each chapter. The questions are there to help you process not only what you learned in the chapter, but how it made you feel and it's meant to help you move forward on your journey as you "Get Off Your Ash".

Chapter 1—Worksheet

Has anything that happened to Job ever happened to you (i.e. – loss of a loved one, loss of income or a means of income, etc.)? If so, list those things that you now realize have contributed to the pile of ash you're sitting on below?

____

____

What was your reaction in the moment of loss?

____

____

What has your reaction been after some time has passed?

____

____

Have you been afraid to get off your ash and move forward? Do you find you've become comfortable in the pain and hurt?

____

____

Are there coping mechanisms you've put into place in order to deal with the ash? If so, what are they?

____

____

How has going through this "ash-full" experience changed or affected you?

____

____

Have you ever allowed another person's opinion of you to shape or affect who you are? If so, how?

____

____

Has sitting on your ash robbed you of the joy in your life or prevented you from pursuing your passion? If so, what has it prevented you from doing?

____

____

Chapter 2
MOVE YOUR ASH

◇◇◇◇◇◇◇

I will die with my nest,
and I will live as long as a phoenix.
—Job 29:18 (CJB)

◇◇◇◇◇◇◇

Okay! Well, that's a weird thing to see in a Bible verse, right? A phoenix? Really? Yup. There it is in black and white. Did you know that the phoenix has been used as a Christian symbol of the resurrection since the first century? Yup. I just said that. In fact, a quick Google search will confirm what I have just said. Why in the world would certain Bible translations choose to use the word "phoenix"—a mythical bird…of pagan origin…in the Holy Bible. That's a good question. Thankfully, there's an equally good answer.

The legend of the phoenix exists in one form or another in various ancient cultures. The stories vary from region to region, but essentially, they all tell the same story. The phoenix was said to be a bird equal in size to an eagle. However, unlike an eagle, or any other bird for that matter, the phoenix was said to live for five hundred years. As it approached the end of its life, it would make a nest, burst into flames, and would burn until only a pile of ash was left. Soon after its fiery death, it would transform back to life. It would literally rise out of the ashes. And so, the phoenix is locked into an eternal loop of death and resurrection, of a life reborn anew and transformed. It literally became a new creature. You can see how and why the early church fathers made the connection between the phoenix and the resurrection.

It's worthwhile noting which early Church fathers drew a comparison between the phoenix and the resurrection of Jesus: Clement, Origen, Tertullian, Ambrose, Cyril of Jerusalem, and Jerome. If you wish to learn more about what they said, their quotes are readily available online. There's even a 13th century mosaic of a phoenix from Old St. Peter's Basilica in Rome on display at the Museo di Roma. Just to clarify, Old St. Peter's Basilica was the original building that stood from the 4th to 16th centuries and it's where the new St. Peter's Basilica stands today in Vatican City. That's right, the parallels between the phoenix and Christ, made it all the way to the Vatican. So, why in the world are we even talking about this?

Job thought he would live forever. He thought that his life would remain in an eternal state of perfection. When he recounts his thoughts in Job 29:18, his life was going great. People respected him. Some even feared him. He was revered by his peers. I think that if Job had the power to take the perfect snapshot of his life and freeze it to hold it up as a memorial of how great his life was…it would be this moment. As we previously discussed, just like the burning of bodies were common place during Job's lifetime, so was the story of the phoenix. Not only did Job want to live forever, he wanted to live forever perfectly.

Job sat on his ash, dreaming about the glory days, and in doing so, was in denial about his current circumstances. Come on…we've all "pulled a Job". How many times have we found ourselves going down memory lane when our lives are going down the tubes? It makes us feel better to think about and dwell on the good times of the past.

There's nothing wrong with remembering or celebrating past achievements or special moments. The danger comes when we start spending more time in the past than we do in the present. When we're dealing with the pain and trauma of the present, the past can offer seductive but only temporary relief. Allow your pain to refine you… not define you.

This is the lesson I wish I had learned back in 2015, when the painful memories of my past first began to emerge. The inability to learn and grow from difficult circumstances is one of the leading causes of why many people continually remain sitting on their proverbial ashes. I know I did. Allow me to speak from personal experience on this one. I'm not a behavioral analyst. I'm not an expert in cognitive therapy. What I am is…a survivor. I know what it's like to sit on your ash. Ash, as a metaphor for pain, grief and loss, is quite appropriate.

I Got Off My Ash

I sat on my ash for a solid five years. My ash and I have had a love/hate relationship ever since

I can remember. I've been down and defeated many times, but I always got back up. After the childhood sexual abuse memories started coming back, it became increasingly harder and harder to get off my ash.

Why did I stay there? Why do any of us stay there? Because it provides us with a distorted and unnatural sense of comfort. Leaving the ash behind you is hard. It's terrifying. As horrible and miserable of an experience it is, at least you know what to expect. At first, the pain is overwhelming and insufferable. But given enough time, it slowly becomes a part of you. It sadistically starts to modify your behavior and personality. And for some inexplicable reason, we will often contend with the power of darkness to stay on our ash. We're going to continue exploring this relationship that we have with pain and suffering. But right now, let me give you a glimpse of what a life off your ash can look like.

The year was 1991. I was happy. Really happy. I had been married to the love of my life for about a year. We had bought our first home. We were both pretty fulfilled where we were working. Life was good. I wasn't prone to having big dreams or aspirations. I just wanted to be married, make enough money to pay my bills, and enjoy life with friends and family. I'm sure that many of you who are reading this can relate. Wake up. Go to work. Come home. Have dinner. Watch TV. Go to sleep. Wake up and do it all over again the next day. And the next day. And the next…

Everything was going just like it had been going pretty much every day…until. Until I woke up from one of the most vivid and realistic dreams I had ever had up to that point in my life. As I close my eyes and think back to the dream, I can still picture it now. In the dream, I was in an SUV of some type. I remember driving through some pretty thick brush. I could hear branches scraping up against the side of the vehicle. It was hot—really hot. There were some other passengers in the car with me. I couldn't make out who they were, but I knew that I wasn't alone in the car and that I didn't know them that well. After what seemed to be a very long and bumpy drive, the thick green color of the trees gave way, and we came to a clearing. It was an open area with dusty paths.

And then, I don't know how or where they came from, but a large group of children started following behind the vehicle. They were African. They were singing, or maybe chanting something. I couldn't make out what they were saying, but they were happy—infectiously so. They were running after the car and they had their arms stretched out to me. It's like they were expecting to receive something from me, but I didn't have anything to give them. I felt so bad, but I wasn't prepared. I thought I was just going for a ride; I didn't know we were on our way to see so many children. And just like that, I woke up and the dream was over.

I remember feeling very confused by the dream. Why were these children following me and why were they expecting me to give them something? I was so sad that I couldn't help them. I tucked it away and didn't think about it again for a long time. Let's fast forward twenty-eight years later to 2019. My son Daniel and I were on our way to Liberia in West Africa. (Don't worry...there will be an entire chapter devoted to how I ended up serving in Africa just after my 49th birthday.) In order to show you what a life off your ash can look like, let's just start with me going to Liberia. I knew my life had changed the moment we landed.

As you will learn later, I spent many years travelling around the world. My career as an itinerant teacher took me to some pretty amazing places and I met some pretty incredible people along the way. I have been to Hong Kong several times. I was able to travel to places like Australia and England and South Africa. I went to Israel more than forty times, but more on that later. Even though I had amazing experiences in these other countries, I never felt compelled to move there or devote the rest of my life to just one country or people. But that is exactly what happened when I went to Liberia for the first time.

I was asked to speak at several events in and around the capital city of Monrovia, in a subdivision called Paynesville. My son and I brought seven suitcases filled with toothpaste, toothbrushes, soap, medical supplies and small toys for the children at a school we would be visiting. The pastor who invited me to Liberia was in charge of setting my itinerary for this two-week trip. He had scheduled lots of teaching sessions as well as visiting some local schools and medical clinics. I can't tell you why, but of all the things that were being planned, I asked if there would be any way for us to go visit a village in what we would call the jungle. I figured if we were going all the way over to Africa, it would be pretty cool to see what life in a remote village looked like.

So, they arranged for us to go visit this community called Kartoe Town—a small, remote village in Margibi County, about three hours away from where we were staying. I decided to buy a few bales of clothing for the children of the village. We were told that we were the first outsiders to be given permission to come visit them, so I didn't want to show up empty-handed.

So, we drove, and drove, and drove. The car broke down a couple of times on the way. The air conditioning was kind of working, but it still was pretty warm in the truck. The "roads" were in pretty rough shape. We got stuck a few times. We had to keep getting out of the vehicle in order to lighten the load enough for the car to pass through some pretty rough terrain. The roads were getting more and more bumpy. They got more and more narrow the deeper into the jungle we travelled. Branches were scraping up against the sides and roof of the vehicle. It was almost as if I had been there before...

As we entered the village, I felt like I was dreaming. It looked like so many small villages I had seen on TV. The difference this time was, I was actually there. The main square had a few dozen homes. They were very simple—mostly made out of mud bricks and salvaged wood, and a thatched roof comprised of a mixture of palm and bamboo leaves. Some people had fires going with large pots filled with rice. Others were seeking shelter from the blistering heat by sitting in the shade being cast by some local tropical trees. It was all so simple, and at the same time, it was all so beautiful. They don't get a lot of visitors, so we were definitely the talk of the town that day. People smiled and waved as we continued to drive to the main courtyard.

All of a sudden, I heard a commotion coming from behind us. I turned my head to look over my shoulder and was shocked by what I was seeing. A group of children were running behind the car. I couldn't make out what they were saying, but they were very enthusiastic. I decided to put my window down and couldn't believe what I was seeing and hearing. They were singing and clapping as they ran. There were about thirty of them. I pulled my phone out and just started recording.

Now that a couple of years have passed since my first visit to this village, I can't believe that I didn't make the connection sooner. It was May 3, 2019 and they were singing, "Jehovah, you are a mountain remover!" The children kept singing and running along the vehicle until we reached the main hall. We unloaded the bales of clothing and spent the next few hours distributing it to the kids.

We would hold up an outfit and then would look for a child who we thought the clothing would best fit. Once we started giving out the clothing, more and more kids kept coming. They were so excited. Most of them had never received a gift before, and certainly not from an outsider who looked like me! They kept raising their hands to receive an outfit. It didn't matter if the clothes were too big; they knew how rare this all was and it meant so much to them.

We spent a few hours talking to the elders and various families around the village. They showed us some of their agricultural areas. They showed us how they tapped the rubber trees and talked about how they would take it to the market in the city to sell. We played soccer with the children. It was truly a remarkable experience.

That first trip still registers as some of the best and most fulfilling days of my life. Annnd...none of it would have happened if I had just stayed home and sat on my ash. If I had continued sulking about what had happened to me in the past. If I had just wallowed in my sorrows and kept the pity-party going. I would have missed all of it. I've had so many people tell me that my story has encouraged them; that my journey to step out of my comfort zone has helped them to do the same. But here's the thing…I had to step out. I had to risk going to a country I had never been to before, to meet with people I had never met before. I would have nothing to write about if I hadn't gotten off of my ash.

We get stuck like Job. The pain is real. The hurt is real. The memories are real. We add all of these feelings and emotions to our ash pile. And when we sit on it long enough, we become comfortable—too comfortable. We're inmates in a self-made prison and we don't even know it. Some people don't even realize they have been wearing chains until they decide to move. It's okay to be hurt. It's okay to feel betrayed, broken and bruised. But it's not okay to sit there and do nothing. It's not okay to miss out on all that life has to offer.

We have to get up. We have to get off our ash. If we don't go, we won't grow. This is where the analogy of the phoenix comes back. Yes, the phoenix sat in its nest. Yes, the phoenix was consumed by fire. Yes, the phoenix was reduced to a pile of ash. But its journey didn't end there did it? No. It was reborn out of its own ashes.

There are some profound similarities between the experience of this legendary bird and our own lives. It's good to note that the bird wasn't moved to a new nest in order to be reborn. No, its ash, its journey, became the foundation for its new life. It's the exact same way with us. You don't have to have a perfect past or a perfect life in order to live a perfectly content life. We can actually use all the ash that we have collected over a lifetime. It's the ash that makes us who we are. Everything we have ever been through has added to—not taken away from—who or what we have become.

I love this quote from BJ Neblett:

> We are the sum total of our experiences. Those experiences – be they positive or negative – make us the person we are, at any given point in our lives. And, like a flowing river, those same experiences, and those yet to come, continue to influence and reshape the person we are, and the person we become. None of us are the same as we were yesterday, nor will be tomorrow.

Life is going to knock you down. Get back up. It doesn't matter if you get knocked down one time or ten times or a hundred times. You get back up. Just like the phoenix, you are going to use everything you have been through to come out stronger and more resilient. Every experience that tried to destroy you can only destroy you if you let it. I know that when you're on fire, it hurts and it feels like an eternity. But know that the fire will end, the ash will come, and then…you will rise!

I've used everything in my ash to become a better person. I no longer allow my past to dictate my present or my future. I channel the pain. I turn what used to be ugly into something beautiful. I write books. I produce television. I travel the world and, by the grace of God, I'm transforming lives. And none of that would have happened if I sat around on my ash all day feeling sorry for myself.

It doesn't matter who did what to us, or when they did it. What matters is now. Today. We can use the elements of our ash to set us free and propel us towards greatness, or we can use it to remain in shackles. We can live in fear of what others will say, or we can live a life of freedom. I don't know about you, but I'm choosing freedom. Freedom today. Freedom tomorrow. Live, fly, die, repeat—the story of the phoenix. Let it be your story too. It's time to get off your ash! It's time to move your ash.

Chapter 2—Worksheet

Have you ever "pulled a Job"—dwelling on the past so much that it's affecting your present? If so, what are the things you think about often and lament over their loss or pain?

____

____

What significant events in your life have shaped you and made you who you are—good or bad?

____

____

Have you found that the good things or the painful things have had more of an affect on you?

____

____

What, if anything, has kept you in "prison"? I.e. - The opinions of others? Fear? Your past?

____

____

Chapter 3
TAKE YOUR HEAD OUT OF YOUR ASH

For there is hope for a tree, if it be cut down,
that it will sprout again, and that its shoots will
not cease. Though its root grow old in the earth, and
its stump die in the soil, yet at the scent of water it
will bud and put out branches like a young plant.
—Job 14:7-9 (ESV)

How would you define worry? One online dictionary puts it this way—"give way to anxiety or unease; allow one's mind to dwell on difficulty or troubles." The second half of that definition really resonates with me and with what I'm trying to get across in this book. As long as you live your life with your heart and mind continually in the past, you will never be able to fully enjoy living in the present, and you will also find it difficult to envision a happy future. The longer we obsess and focus on those things that happened to us, it becomes increasingly more difficult to dream about what might happen to and through us.

One of the things I get asked about most often is, how was I able to accomplish some of the things in my life. I've been blessed to be able to be a part of some pretty incredible things. I never really knew how to articulate or explain the process I went through. Until now. Now, I can clearly and honestly walk you through the process of how I have been able to do what I have done. I got off my ash. It's so simple that it is incredibly profound.

Let's take another quick look at what the ash represents and how sitting on it, remaining in it, continually thinking about it, can have a detrimental and negative impact on our lives. They say that the things that really matter, never come easily. That it takes hard work, effort and commitment. But I would also add at least one more thing to that list. It starts with a decision. It starts with a yes. People asked me how I ended up travelling to Malaysia, an Islamic Republic, many times. I said yes to the invitation. In fact, it was at a church in Petaling Jaya that I had one of the most powerful encounters with God in my entire life. The other was at the City of Light church in Barnersville, Liberia.

I've entitled this chapter, "Take Your Head Out of Your Ash". Again, it's more than just a clever play on words. There is a life changing message behind it. Sometimes we can get so focused on and distracted by our past grievances, as well as our current circumstances, that we can't see past them. We can't envision a future filled with hope and expectation because we continually focus on a past filled with despair and dread. We often miss out on what could have been because of what has been. It's an awful way to live, but many of us fall into this default position because we have been so used to sitting on our collective ashes.

So, the ash that I speak of in this book refers to some of the dark and difficult times that you may have experienced in the past. It could be the loss of a loved one. It could be a failed marriage. A friendship that you thought would go the distance, but instead, ended up in the agony of betrayal. It could also be a business idea that you thought for sure was going to change the world…and your life.

Whatever it was, it seemingly crashed and burned. And all that remains is a hot, smoking pile of ash. And then you went and sat on it. Don't worry, I sat on it too. Why do we do this to ourselves?

Let me tell you as honestly and as simply as I can…you will never be able to move forward with anything until you take your head out of your ash. All your ash does is keep you prisoner. The ash fills you with fear and reminds you of failure. It's paralyzing, debilitating and humiliating. Yet, for some sick and twisted reason, we choose to sit there. Some of us have even lived there for years at a time. I know that getting off your ash can seem like a daunting and scary thing to do, but I promise you, it's the best thing you will ever do for yourself.

Once you take your head out of your ash, meaning, that you will not continually default to going there in your mind when something goes wrong or gets scary, you will be on the cusp of launching out into a future that you never dreamed was possible. As you take your head out of the ash, the chains that bind you will loose and you will be free to move into a whole new realm of existence—an existence where you are no longer controlled by fear or rejection. You will enjoy a future that is worth getting up for in the morning. Are you ready for it?

Again, I'm speaking from experience here. I sat on my ash for a long time. It's frustrating to think about how much time I lost because I decided to sit and sulk in the ash. To put it plainly, I was "pulling a Job". I'm glad to be able to tell you, that although I still have moments when sitting on my old ash is tempting, I've overcome it by taking my head out of my ash and focusing on what could be done, not what has been done. That type of thinking is a game-changer. The heavens are opened, the fog is lifted, and a new day and season arises. Let me give you a personal example. It happened in 2005, but we'll have to go back to 2002 for context.

2002 marked the tenth anniversary of my time in ministry. I had served in various roles and in different cities around the greater Toronto area. I had just resigned from a small church I had been pastoring in a little placed called Victoria Harbour, about two hours north of Toronto. It was a beautiful small town on the shores of Georgian Bay. It was a fisherman's dream come true. I truly loved the people in our church and community. The church was growing and as a church, we were really starting to make a name for ourselves. Then, seemingly out of the blue, I just up and resigned. All of a sudden, out of nowhere, I just felt done.

At the time, I didn't know why I wanted to leave. I just felt like I had to. I remember the word picture I gave to my wife to help her understand what was going on inside of me. I felt like a car with an engine that was about to overheat and potentially explode. I knew that if I didn't pull over right away, I would cause a lot of unnecessary damage.

So, I called an emergency board meeting. I informed them of my decision, and two weeks later, I was gone. Just like that. I wasn't aware of it at the time, but my mind and body were starting to become subconsciously aware of the traumatic childhood sexual abuse I had gone through, but my mind wasn't ready to deal with it. This abrupt change was very difficult for our young family.

To cut a very long story short, during that time of "in-between", I ended up being sponsored to go to Israel. I never had a desire to go, but when it came up, I decided to go. It turns out that it was the very thing I needed, even if I wasn't aware of it. That first trip awoke something in me that I didn't even know existed. There was a writer inside of me. There was a researcher and a history buff.

I would spend the next twenty years becoming an expert in understanding the Hebraic roots of the Christian faith. I worked closely with the local Israeli archaeological community. I got to see and touch things from the First Century, from the time of Jesus, I got to do things that I never dreamed I would be a part of.

When I returned home from my third trip in 2004, an idea entered into my head that, to this day, I can't believe I had. Once I started making a bit of a name for myself as a first century Bible expert, invitations started coming my way. I began travelling across the country speaking at churches, camps and conferences. And then came the invitation that changed my life—an invitation to be interviewed on a Christian TV talk show. I remember flying out from Toronto, Ontario to Calgary, Alberta, then driving another few hours south until we reached the city of Lethbridge, Alberta. I pulled into the parking lot and I can still remember being scared to death.

What could I possibly have to say that would warrant my voice, and face, going out across the country! But yet, there I was. It was called "The Miracle Channel". Again, I didn't know it at the time, but I was getting off my ash. I was getting out of my comfort zone and was stepping out into a whole new platform that scared the life out of me. But…I did it. In fact, that host who interviewed me said I was really good at it. He even called me a natural. I was blown away. I never dreamed in my life that I would be on TV, let alone be good at it.

I like to say that I fell in love that day. That is, I fell in love with that red light on the camera. When that light was on, it meant that millions of people had the opportunity to learn what I had been learning. It went so well that they flew me back out the very next week to film an entire week of segments for them. That was the turning point in my career as an itinerant speaker. There is no doubt about it. I remember flying back home after taping all those shows with a crazy little idea in my head— "I should be on TV more often!" Can you imagine the audacity?

I did a bit of research and started putting together a budget of what it would cost to purchase a couple of cameras, hire a small crew, and rent some studio space. It was only going to cost a mere $200,000 or so. Big deal, right? I shared this amazing, fool-proof plan with my dear wife. She encouraged me in my gifting and agreed that I was being called to be on television so that many others would be able to learn about all the things I had been learning. She also reminded me that we had no money. And then she said something that shocked me to my core. She told me that when it was time for me to start my own TV show, that God would provide every penny of it in advance. Do you want to know what this holy and faith-filled man thought when she told me that? The answer is disappointing but honest. I said to myself, "Great, I guess I'll never be on TV." I told you…disappointing, but true.

I've never told this story on such a public platform before, but I think it's important for me to share this in order to encourage some of you out there who are discouraged and struggling to make your ideas become a reality.

I don't remember exactly how much time had passed since the incident of my shockingly lack-of-faith-on-display, but the unimaginable happened. In early 2004, I started working with the largest Jewish travel agency in Canada to help me build what became my annual tour to Israel.

Over the years, I took dozens of tours to Israel to walk through the land of the Bible and in Jesus' footsteps. I honestly and earnestly believed that visiting the land of the Scriptures would be of great benefit for every person who considered themselves to be a follower of Christ. Seeing the places where He taught and healed people was worth more than any price you could ever pay to join a tour.

I remember telling the owner of the travel agency that if we could somehow show all of the incredible Bible locations of Israel on TV to Christians, that tourism could grow exponentially. He agreed. Not only did he agree, but he encouraged me to start a weekly TV program that would teach Christians about the Bible and end with a pitch to bring them on tour with me to Israel. I told him that it was great idea, but that I didn't have the money to pull off such a venture.

Without telling me, he approached the Israel Ministry of Tourism (IMOT) on my behalf. He told them about my idea to produce a weekly Christian Television show whose end-goal, in part, would be to bring as many Christians as possible to Israel. As you could imagine, they loved the idea too. So, they called a meeting.

Next thing I know, I'm making a PowerPoint presentation to a room filled with Jewish Israelis that it would be a great idea for them to help me pay for a TV show that would talk about Jesus. Not only did they think it was a great idea; not only did they agree to partially fund the program, but IMOT and the Jewish travel agency combined their resources and agreed to cover 100% of the expenses to create and broadcast my TV show across the country!

I don't say this enough, but my wife was right. It happens a lot more often than I would like to admit sometimes, but she was right. She was 100% right. God came through and fully funded the launch of the television program. I hosted and produced that show for ten years. It took a few years of hard work, commitment and determination, but that show more than carried itself and helped deepen the faith of many Christians. Why am I telling you all this?

It's hard to tell a story like that without sounding like a giant megalomaniac, I know. But honestly, although I'm very proud of what I was able to accomplish through that TV show, the real reason why I shared the story of its genesis, is to encourage you and to demonstrate what can happen when you are willing to get off your ash.

I'd like to remind you that just a few years before this, I felt like a car whose engine was on fire and was about to explode. And now, a short time later, I had a hit weekly TV show. I'd like to also remind you that, other than having done a few TV interviews, I had no blessed idea what I was doing. I simply had a passion and a desire. That was it. I was rewarded, not for my good looks but for my willingness to become comfortable in the uncomfortable.

Talking to someone and sharing an idea with them over dinner is one thing. Texting or emailing an idea is a bit more brazen. But producing, filming and broadcasting a television show, well now, that's in a sense immortality. For better or for worse, most of the shows I produced can still be found online. I'm telling you; those first few years are absolutely cringe-worthy. But I took a chance and stepped out of my comfort zone.

I had had a wonderful young congregation in Victoria Harbour that was growing. I could have stayed there and built a beautiful new church building and established a name for myself in the region. I was comfortable. Looking back now, I was too comfortable, and that was part of the problem.

Earlier, we spoke of the phoenix. The bird who would live and die in a blaze of fire, only to be reborn out of its own ashes. That's what I want for you. That's what I want this chapter to instill in you—that it doesn't matter how many times you crash and burn, there's always an opportunity to rise again. Not from some Hollywood perfect life. No. But you can rise out of the very ashes you just came from. I want you to understand and accept that those things that were done to you were not your fault. You didn't cause it and you didn't deserve it. We accept what happened. We accept the consequences of our actions as a result of the trauma we endured, and then…we move on.

Even though you were once down. Even though you may have been bruised in the process, you are not broken. I know that in my own experience I still carry the scars of my past. My human nature is to return to the pain of my ash as a default. It's something that I have been working on for many years now. I'm not where I want to be, but I thank God that I'm not where I used to be. You and I will never be able to move on if we are continually going back to sit on our ash, because it's familiar, or because it's comfortable.

All those years of producing television, writing books, and travelling the world, it almost never happened. It almost never happened because I always felt inadequate or insecure. My past experience—my ash—told me that I wasn't good enough. The pain in my ash tried to convince me that I wasn't worthy of success or had value, that I would never be the best at anything…so why even try. And because of this, we shrink back, and what do we do? We go back to sitting on our ash.

You see, when you feel rejected, you act rejected. You see and hear things through the lens of how you're feeling or what you're going through. People never really have a chance of making a deep connection with you. Because you were betrayed, burned and cheated, without thinking about it, you automatically put up walls to make sure it never happens again. You didn't have control over what happened to you, so now you do everything to make sure that you're the one in charge of what happens to you.

This behaviour can cause people to shrink back from us, and as a result, we end up feeling alone and abandoned. And what do we do when we start feeling this way? Yup. You guessed it. We go back to sitting on our ash. It's a vicious cycle. So how do we break it? It starts with us. The battle begins and ends in our minds.

When I launched out with a weekly television show, I was so scared. I wasn't scared of the camera. Talking to the lens was the easy part. I was scared of what people would say when they saw me on TV. Would they be able to tell that I didn't know what I was doing? Would they be able to sense the deep fear of rejection that I was so desperately trying to hide?

I just kept going. Episode after episode. Season after season. Year after year. I came to the place in my career where I was acting confident, because I felt confident. I had to fight every day. I had to fight the negative feelings and image that I had of myself. I had to stop allowing my past to define and dictate who I am today. I had to get my head out of my ash.

You know what? I'm still fighting today. I'm fighting, even as I write these words, I'm fighting. But that's okay. I will not allow my ash to hold me down. I will not allow the negative experiences of my past to destroy or taint the joy that I can experience today. I'm passionate about what I do. I love what I do, and I believe in what I am doing. And if I can help just one person on their journey, then that is something that's worth fighting for. When you sit on your ash, you're not just hurting yourself. You're not just robbing yourself. You're also robbing the world around you of what you have to offer. Don't you dare sit on your ash.

What's the dream? What's the life altering idea that's floating around in your brain? Why haven't you acted on it? If the answer is your ash…it's time to do something about it. If you're ready…it's time to leave your ash behind.

Chapter 3—Worksheet

Are there things you have perhaps missed out on because you were focused on the past? If so, what things?

____

____

What would you prefer to focus on to get your head out of your ash?

____

____

Are there things you have become too comfortable in that you don't want to risk becoming uncomfortable? If so, what are they?

____

____

What bruises or scars from your past do you carry?

____

____

Have you pulled back from a relationship or an opportunity because of fear of rejection? If so, is there any particular person or situation that comes to mind?

____

____

What's your dream or idea that has been floating around in your brain?

____

____

Why haven't you acted on it?

____

____

Chapter 4
LEAVE YOUR ASH BEHIND

◇◇◇◇◇◇◇

Agree with God, and be at peace;
thereby good will come to you.
—Job 22:21 (ESV)

◇◇◇◇◇◇◇

One of the greatest tragedies I have encountered over the years is when people choose to pre-fail. What does that mean you might be asking? It's when someone has already determined in their own minds that they are going to fail miserably at whatever it is that they are about to do. No way, you say. Why in the world would anyone do that to themselves? The answer is quite simple actually: it's because they haven't been able to leave their ash behind.

We've talked about what sitting on your ash for too long does to a person. They get so used to the pain, rejection, fear and failure of the ash that they don't know how to function without it. They're almost afraid to get rid of or deal with the pain of the ash. Those negative feelings are actually quite powerful. It's almost as if they leave an imprint on your soul.

For some people, no matter what they do or how hard they try, they are unable to shake off the negative and pessimistic feelings. Have you ever met someone like that? Maybe you *are* someone like that. The sun can be shining; not a cloud in the sky; there's a beautiful breeze; and all they can do is complain about the dangers of UV radiation and how the government has failed to protect them. And you're left there just scratching your head.

Now, I obviously made up the last scenario, but it's probably not too far off from some real-life situations that you have experienced. I don't think I've ever blamed the government for too much sun, but I definitely know what it is like to carry around negative feelings and thoughts about myself. These awful thoughts about myself didn't happen naturally. They stem from bad experiences that I had as a teenager.

I was once told by a person who was supposed to be my leader, that I would never amount to anything. This person berated me in front of a large group. I was mortified, to say the least. At the time, I wasn't aware of the impact that incident would have on my life. I struggled with low self-esteem for decades because of what happened that day. I can't believe how long I carried that ash around with me. Even now, as I'm writing this, it still stings a little bit.

When people who know me read this, they won't believe it. I've always come across as being so bold and confident. The truth is, there is a hurt and terrified little boy living inside of me. I've had to work really hard at leaving my ash behind. And, if I get too comfortable for too long, the pain of my ash comes back. I'm telling you—when it hits, it can knock you so hard that it's disorienting. You don't know which way is up. You can feel dazed and confused. Some people can shake it off and get back up, but for most of us, it can take days, months, years, or even decades.

I know too many people who are smart and talented, who have self-sabotaged. I have someone in my life who is very dear to me, and I've watched them struggle for years because they have found it difficult to leave their ash behind. Like them, the voice in our head is the most powerful one and the one we most often listen to. In your mind, you have already failed, so why even bother trying? What will others think? That negative and destructive voice in our head is so loud, that it drowns out everything else, even the voice of reason. Why do we behave this way? Why do we put ourselves through such constant and consistent pain? It's like we have a dysfunctional codependency with the pain in our ash! Only when we decide to leave the pain of our ash behind, can we truly move forward.

Let me ask you a question, but I need you to answer honestly. Don't tell me or other people what you think they want to hear, but rather, tell the honest and naked truth. So, here's the question. What's your biggest fear about getting off your ash and pursuing a goal or desire that you have in your heart? Seriously. What's the worst thing that can happen? I'm not speaking about the financial aspect of a business launch or investment; I'm talking about going after the dream that you've had in your heart since you were a child.

Maybe for you, it's to start painting or perhaps you've been wanting to start a cooking blog, or launch a YouTube channel. So, again, I ask, what's the worst thing that can happen if you completely flop? I mean, failing in an epic fashion. Don't worry, I'm not asking you a question that I haven't asked myself. I have tried many things in my life. Sometimes it was awesome and was a huge success. Other times, not so much. We need to learn to celebrate our successes and failures in equal measure. That's how we grow.

Let me tell you something that I have learned in my fifty-one years of being on this earth: it's only a failure if you didn't learn from it. If you learned something from the experience, then it was a lesson. Every so-called failure taught you what not to do next time. The act of not succeeding can serve as an exceedingly important and valuable lesson.

There are things that I have done in my life that would be considered a colossal failure by some. But that's not true. Learning what not to do can be just as important as knowing what to do. I have seen this play out in my own life many times. Think of each decision you make as a stepping stone towards where you are heading on your journey.

I've already told you about what it was like to get off my ash and launch a weekly television program. I'm telling you…even though it was the most difficult and scariest thing I had done in my life up to that point, I'm so glad I did it. I wouldn't change a thing about that experience. That season in my life has led to some other extraordinary opportunities. When I first started that show, I had no idea what would happen. I hoped that people would watch it, but I didn't know for sure. One of the main reasons for starting the show was to encourage people to make a pilgrimage to Jerusalem. It worked. It really worked. We had so many people calling in to sign up for one of our tours to Israel. Not only could they walk where Jesus walked, but they could see what He saw too. We were offering people the opportunity to see and hear what Jesus really meant.

We took bus-loads of people over the years. The Israel Ministry of Tourism (IMOT) got wind of how well the tours were going. I didn't even know they were paying attention. Turns out that this little show from Milton, Ontario, Canada was having more of an impact than I ever imagined.

In fact, IMOT was so impressed, that in February of 2012, they bestowed a very prestigious honor on me. They awarded me the "Faithful Ambassador Award" during the National Religious Broadcasters (NRB) conference in Nashville, Tennessee with over 1000 pastors from around the world present.

It was an amazing moment. There were a lot of well-known people in the room that day. Many people in the same field aspire to receive this award. I honestly wasn't looking for it, but nonetheless, I was humbled by it. Again, why would I recount this story from my life? Because it never would have happened if I wasn't willing to get off my ash and pursue the ideas in my heart.

Most people spend years in school studying and preparing for their respective careers. People will spend years climbing the corporate ladder: always looking for the next promotion; always having their eye on that corner office; hoping for that salary bump and all the benefits that come with it. And I get it. I really do. But, to me, that sounds absolutely awful! The thought of being at the same place doing the same thing with the same people for years on end…well, let's just say that doesn't appeal to me at all. Most people dream of getting to a place in their careers where things are on auto-pilot, where things have been put in place and just run themselves. For me, that was a nightmare.

As I've already said, I've been fortunate to be a part of some pretty amazing things in my life. Swimming with dolphins in the Red Sea with my family is not something that most people can say, but I got to do that. I also swam in a bay in Australia which is the most densely populated area for baby great white sharks. Not sure why I did that, but I did. Now, before you create some scenario in your head of how brave I was to do such a thing, let me paint a much less flattering, yet truthful order of events. Our host pastor kept telling me that I had come all the way to Australia from Canada, and that I had to go into the shark infested water. I had zero intention of doing this. I don't know if it was his Aussie accent or what, but I finally caved and went in. Not just up to my ankles or knees. Nope, all the way up to my chest.

Because of all the sharks in the area, the beach patrol was pretty intense. They had lifeguards on watchtowers looking for shadows in the water. They had fenced off a small swimming area with steel meshing, and they had helicopters patrolling the area as well. I kind of felt safe, but the theme music from the movie JAWS kept playing louder and louder in my head. And just as I was starting to feel confident…it happened. Something touched my leg, and the most unnatural, fierce, and unmanly screech came out of my mouth. And I swam and ran back to shore as fast as my almost paralyzed-by-fear body would allow me to. However, I lived to tell the story. I guess there is one small detail of that event that I have left out. I'd love to say that I had a brush with death as I stared down a fierce great white shark...turns out, it was just a shopping bag floating around in the ocean.

I'll never forget the time I was invited to participate in a live archaeological dig in Migdal, on the western shores of the Sea of Galilee. I had spent several years building a relationship with the lead archaeologist at the time. He invited me to join him as the team was unearthing and surveying a new section of this abandoned 2000-year-old fishing village.

Just being there was awesome. But it got better, way better. I was walking around the site just trying to take in where I was. I mean, this is where the famous Mary Magdalene was from. So much history had happened here. The lead archeologist motioned for me to go to where he was. As I arrived, he was unearthing a jar that was being seen by human eyes for the first time in over 2000 years. It was truly an amazing experience. Please remember why I'm sharing these stories with you. It's to remind you a what a life can look like once you choose to get off your ash.

I could literally write an entire book filled with all the crazy and amazing experiences I've had because I was willing to get out of my comfort zone, off my ash, and risk living a life where I didn't have full control over everything that may or may not happen to me. What if I had chosen to sit on my ash because I was afraid of what people might say about me? What if I allowed the worry of judgment and rejection control me? What if I allowed the fear of failure to dictate what I would or would not do? I would have missed out on so much because of what a few people may or may not have thought about me. Missing out on life because of what others might say or do about you is no way to live at all.

I would have missed out on so much if I had given in to fear and stayed on my comfortable ash. I would have missed out on going to Thailand, Malaysia, Singapore, Hong Kong, China, Australia, England, Italy, South Africa, almost every province in Canada and several states in America. You will never be able to move forward until you are willing to let go of the pain and hurt from your past.

Let me give you another example from my own life. I love boating. There's something about being on a boat. The throttle down. The wind in your hair (whatever's left of mine, anyways). The beauty of the shoreline. The smell of the fresh air. And I love the silence. I love it when you go full speed to the center of the lake, turn off the engine. Just let the momentum of the waves carry you for a few feet. Then, absolute silence. Just the gentle sound of the waves breaking against the side of the boat.

I've been blessed to own a small boat or two in the past. My love for boating started when I was in Bible College. We lived about two hours north of Toronto in a place called Peterborough. My favourite part about living there was the fact that we were surrounded by dozens of small lakes, rivers and waterways. During the warmer months, I would be out on the water almost every day. I loved driving out to the lake as the sun was coming up. Catching a bass or two in the morning. It was a great way to start off the day.

Whether you have a $1500 or $15,000 boat, there is one thing that is always the same. No matter how many horsepower your motor has. No matter how many people you can seat. All boaters have to do the same thing in order to get going: if you're at the dock, you have to untie the boat and if you're out on the lake, you have to take up your anchor. There's no way around it.

If you're at the dock and still have the boat tied to the dock, it doesn't matter how much you try or how hard you press on the throttle, if you're still tied up, you're not going anywhere! In fact, you'll either damage the boat as you try to pull away, or, you risk blowing the motor all together or wrecking your dock.

Same thing when you are out in the middle of the water. If you forget to pull up the anchor before you hit the throttle, you'll blow the engine. You might be able to move a few feet, but the end result will be the same, your boat will be completely useless without a motor, and then you will be stuck out in the middle of nowhere!

It's the same thing in life. You can't move forward—at least, not efficiently—while still being tied to the dock of your past. It's amazing how many people try to move forward in life while they are still tied to the hurt of their past. Burn out, mental breakdowns and anxiety attacks are on the rise. How can you move forward in a relationship when you still haven't dealt with the betrayal or mistrust from the past of a previous relationship?

It's just like the illustration of the boat. You have to untie, or disconnect yourself from the pain of the past if you want to move forward. People are wearing themselves out trying to inch their way forward into the future. People are feeling emotionally burned out and exhausted and they can't understand why.

Friends: it's time to leave your ash behind. Carrying the weight of all that hurt is too much to bear. It's too much to carry. I'm going to suggest something that might seem counter intuitive at first. But stick with me, it will make sense by the end…

I'm a big soccer fan. Not only was I born in Portugal, but I was raised in Canada in a Portuguese home. That means I was raised with all kinds of wonderful food and customs. Family is everything. We did everything together. That first generation of immigrants were close. All of my mother's sisters, husbands and children grew up in the same house. That's just the way it was. No one could afford to have their own place. Everyone pitched in. Not just with the bills but with cooking and cleaning too. It was crazy and chaotic but kind of cool too.

I'm still fluent in Portuguese and somewhat in Spanish because of my upbringing. Not only did growing up in a Portuguese house give me a love of fresh bread and cheese, but I also inherited a love for soccer. Euro Cup and World Cup were huge events for our family. There was always lots of food. My family was loud. They were rowdy. They were awesome.

The love of soccer is still alive and well in me until this very day. My favourite player: Cristiano Ronaldo. Did you even have to ask? I think you can lose your citizenship status if you don't carry a photo of him in your wallet. I may have made that last thing up, but you get it, soccer is important to us. Really important.

I'm a Manchester United supporter. Sorry, but I am. In 2013, I was able to live out a dream that any United soccer fan would understand. I was invited to speak at several church events in Manchester, England. Of course, I had to try to get tickets to see at least one game at Old Trafford, the legendary Manchester United home stadium.

It's nearly impossible to get tickets. As fate would have it, one of the pastors just "happened" to be the official chaplain of the Manchester United Football Club. Can you believe it? I went to two games at Old Trafford, both times it was a capacity crowd of 70,000 fans. It was awesome. I have to be honest; I've been waiting all these years to be able to have a legitimate reason to write about that experience in a book. So why am I writing about it?

Because, soccer is the one sport that perfectly illustrates my conviction of what we need to do in order to move forward. In most sports, the strategy behind the play is to advance towards your opponent's goal. Think of your favourite sport and see if what I am saying is right.

Sometimes, they might go side to side or take the occasional step back. However, in soccer, it is often necessary to go backwards in order to create a goal scoring opportunity. It's quite common actually and happens several times throughout the game. You'll see the team advance forward. If the opposing team's defense has shut you out, instead of moving forward and spoiling the opportunity, the players will often kick the ball backwards. In many cases, they will kick it all the way back to the goalkeeper. The strategy almost always works. You go back, regroup, look for the opening, then attack.

It's the same in life. We have to go backwards in order to be able to go forward. We have to go back and address what happened. We need to face it head-on, full force and deal with the root of the problem. If we try to move into a new relationship or career without dealing with the past, then we become like that boat that is still tied to the dock. We can give it all we got and use all the force we want, but if we're still tied down, we are not going to go anywhere. Unless we are ready to release ourselves from our past and pick up the anchor, we risk blowing the engine and wrecking the entire boat. Your life is too precious to have it destroyed by your past.

I want you to think about the pain in your ash. I want you to name it. I want you to speak to it and tell it that it will no longer hold power over you. I want you to picture in your mind that you are untying yourself from whatever it is that hurt you and has held power over you. Refuse to continue carrying that shame, that hurt, that betrayal, that anger, or whatever it is that has been holding you back.

Then, as you untie yourself, as you bring in that anchor, get ready to hit that throttle and get ready to succeed, to thrive at whatever it is that you have been dreaming of doing. Feel the freedom that comes with letting go of the past. You may not always have calm weather ahead, but you stand a much better chance of surviving the storm when you can outrun it. Get ready. Get set. Go.

Chapter 4—Worksheet

Has anyone ever said something so negative and hurtful to you that it has become part of your pile of ash? If so, what did they say?

____

____

What's your biggest fear about getting off your ash and pursuing a goal or desire that you have in your heart?

____

____

In your mind, what would be the worst possible thing that could happen if you pursue that goal?

____

____

What have past failures taught you? What were the lessons learned?

____

____

Are you "tied to the dock" of your past? If so, how and in what areas?

Chapter 5
HOT ASH

◇◇◇◇◇◇◇◇

But he knows the way that I take;
when he has tried me,
I shall come out as gold.
—Job 23:10 (ESV)

◇◇◇◇◇◇◇◇

Well, I started off this book by talking about Job. We looked at his ash. What was it that he was sitting on? What was it that he was reflecting on and thinking about? What pain, hurt and disappointment was he being consumed by? He lost everything that he held dear. He lost his means of income. He lost all his staff. He lost everything that he had spent a lifetime accumulating. He was the richest man in the entire region. He worked all his life to build an empire that he would one day be able to leave to his children. And then, without warning, every parent's worst fear happened—he lost his children too. Not one by one over the course of many years. Not in a way that he might be able to grieve and accept the loss over time. No…he lost all of his children…at once!

The devastation this news caused Job is absolutely unimaginable. How does any one person process such information? It must have been sensory overload. I'm sure the neurons in his brain were firing in every which way. We over-use the term "calamity" in our culture, but can you think of a better word to describe what receiving that deluge of bad news would feel like? That level of heartbreak would take your breath away and send you into a downward spiral that would be very difficult to recover from.

A calamity is defined as, "an event causing great and often sudden damage or distress; a disaster." All that pain. That anger. That frustration. The disbelief. All of this and more is what comprised the ash that Job was sitting on. It's easy to judge Job and say, "Get off your ash." However, that is a lot easier said than done. Sometimes it takes a minute or two to accept what has happened to us before we can take any steps towards recovery and healing.

We have the advantage of skipping to the last chapter in the book of Job and seeing the outcome. We know that it will be okay. We know that he will heal and that he will recover. We know that he will prosper and that his joy will be restored. But, in that moment, I don't think there was a person on earth who could bring him comfort, no matter how eloquent or educated their words might have been. This is what it says in Job 42:10, "And the LORD restored the fortunes of Job, when he had prayed for his friends. And the LORD gave Job twice as much as he had before."

Job was hurting. He needed to hurt. He needed to process the immense loss that he had just experienced. Job didn't know it. Job didn't believe it. But he would heal. He would smile again. He would be happy again. Why do "bad" things happen to "good" people? It's a question that we have been asking ourselves since anyone can remember. Why does it have to hurt so bad? Why does it take so long to get over pain, hurt and betrayal?

The more I thought about Job's response to the calamity in his life, and his reaction to it, the more

I thought about Newton's Third Law. It says that, "For every action, there is an equal and opposite reaction." Job experienced pain and misery of, well, biblical proportion. Everything he deemed important. Everything that he loved. Gone! Just like that.

His reaction to the devastating news is understandable. But still, why does it have to hurt so bad? Why do things have to get worse before they get better? This process hardly feels fair. Why can't we just skip all the bad stuff, and get to the prize at the end of the day? Why do we have to struggle so much? Why do we have to suffer and carry the weight of disappointment and hurt for such long periods of our lives?

I know that there were a lot of "why" questions in the previous paragraph. But isn't that the truth? Isn't it our instinct to question why something does or does not happen? As humans, don't we always seek to have immediate and total understanding regarding every matter we face? The truth is, there are as many answers as there are questions. In fact, there may be more questions than answers.

I understand that Newton's Law applies to physics, but I also believe that it carries within itself a universal principle as well. I'm not a physics expert by any means. Why even bring that up? Think about it. Here it is again… "For every action, there is an equal and opposite reaction."

What was the "action" that took place in your life? Perhaps it was the betrayal by someone you thought was your friend. Perhaps it was the sudden loss of your job. Think of the power behind either of those actions. Those actions hit you hard.

Often, unless these things have happened to you, it's difficult to comprehend why some people go into such a tail spin after. Some people fall deep into depression. Some people struggle with self-esteem for the rest of their lives. Some people become substance abusers and some become angry. Whatever the reaction is, no matter to what degree, a reaction is not only understandable; it's to be expected. It's literally a law of the universe.

I'm saying this because there are many people who beat themselves up for their reaction to their circumstances. I definitely don't want anyone to sit on their ash, but what I want to do is to help you understand how and why the ash got there in the first place. We've seen it in the life of Job, now let's see a bit more in the life of Joe.

I've said it before, and I'll say it again—2015 was, without a doubt, the worst year of my life. Even though I wasn't initially consciously aware of the actions carried out against me as a young boy, I was most certainly having a strong and equal reaction. I talked about this in the opening chapter of this book. I thought it was over. By "it," I mean my life.

I felt suicidal on and off for about five years. I remember actually thinking about what it would be like. How would I do it? How could it be done in a way that it would work, but also be the least traumatic for whoever would find me? I thought that my family would be better off without me. Once I decided that suicide was definitely not an option, maybe I would just disappear without a trace. I felt like my wife deserved a better husband, I felt that my children deserved a better dad—one who was stronger; one who wasn't damaged goods.

I thought I would never heal. I didn't believe that I would ever recover. I had convinced myself that the only trajectory in my life that was available to me was down. I felt like an airplane whose engines had exploded mid-flight. That we were going down and that there was nothing I could do about it. We were going to crash and all passengers on board would perish with me.

Those five years felt like an eternity. I was living in constant fear of being found out. How would people react when they discovered that Joe Amaral was a survivor of severe and prolonged childhood male sexual abuse? How would they react to learning that I had just been going through the motions of life and ministry?

All those TV episodes I taped. All those services I preached at. All of it. All of it had been done while going through the worst internal pain and struggle I could ever have been in. Would people be mad? Would they feel cheated? How would they react? I felt like a prisoner in my own mind and body. It took time, but I got there. I'm here to tell you that you will too!

I'm going to say something now that some people might not understand. I briefly referred to it in chapter two, but I feel like it's really important to mention it again and expand on it a bit further. As difficult and painful as the process of getting off the ash of sexual abuse was, I'm a more well-rounded person because of it. I know that it may seem counter intuitive at first glance, but I promise you, it's true.

My ability to cope with difficult situations is stronger. I don't react in the same way that many other people do. This has served me well as I have travelled around the world into different cultures and experienced scenarios that were out of my control. The old Joe would have an anxiety attack. The new Joe—the Joe that got off his ash—is a completely different person now. I don't sweat the small stuff anymore.

I feel like my season of healing came at the perfect time in my life. The level of patience and empathy that I received has definitely helped me in where I am currently serving, which is in Liberia, West Africa. I absolutely love working with the people of Liberia. It's a very difficult place to work in. There is extreme poverty. Almost no infrastructure. Running water and flushing toilets are a luxury that most of us have taken for granted. Electricity is scarce, and even when you do have access to it, it's constantly being interrupted. There is no postal service, so forget about online shopping. Oh yeah, and then there is the internet connection. When you can get it, it's slow, choppy, and altogether unreliable.

So, have I sold you on joining me on our next short term missions trip? Probably not. Everything is slower, more expensive, and congested. I've driven in the Middle East and in Europe, but the traffic in Liberia is unlike anything I have ever seen or experienced. Because of the lack of infrastructure, there are currently almost no working stop lights in the capital. Monrovia has over one million inhabitants. Hundreds of thousands of more people come from all over to buy and sell.

Think of the busiest intersection near where you live. Think of how frustrating traffic is during the height of rush hour. Now, imagine all that with no traffic lights. Imagine four people on the back of a motorbike, weaving in and out of traffic lanes. Imagine trucks with corn, or chairs, piled so high, that it seems like the entire vehicle will tip if they take a corner too sharply. Imagine that rush hour is happening as long as the sun is shining.

Welcome to my world. And yes…I love it! I've learned to be patient in traffic. I've learned not to get too upset when someone driving recklessly swipes the side of your car. I've learned to deal with the police at every other intersection who stop you for some trumped up traffic violation. I've learned to deal with going to the bank to withdraw cash, and after hours of waiting, to be told that the bank is out of money for the day. I've learned to wait hours for someone who was supposed to meet you at 8am, and now it's 2pm, and they still haven't shown up and don't answer their phone. And one more for the road: I've had to learn that sometimes we'd show up at a store to pick up an item we'd already paid for, only to be told that they sold it to someone else or that it was stolen overnight.

Are you getting anxious yet? Why have I told you all of these things? Because…if I had not yet dealt with my ash, there is no way that I would be able to continue doing what I am doing. Even though the memories of the abuse are daily. Even though the feelings of inadequacy are ongoing, the process saved me. If I was just content to sit on my ash, to settle for the dulled mediocrity of existence, I never would have been able to do what I do.

The painful process of dying to the past is what has saved me in the present, and what has given me a future. It was hard, painstaking work, but it changed me. It made me who I am today. I will never be grateful for the abuse. However, I am grateful for the process. The intensity of the process is often the driving force behind the progress.

What process do we know about that when the more heat that is applied, the purer the extracted material is? Yup, you guessed it—gold. Everyone loves gold. It's one of the most precious and expensive metals in the world. Like most things in life, many of us are completely unaware of the process of an item and what it takes to get it into our hands.

It's the same thing when it comes to our food. We love a good hamburger or a nice piece of fried chicken, but we don't want to think about what it had to go through before it ended up on our plates. Same goes for fruits or vegetables. We all love to eat them, but we don't want to think about the process.

We even sometimes complain about the price of a product, while we are almost always completely unaware of the incredible effort and energy that had to be put into that final product that we just grab off the shelves at the grocery store.

Gold is a very meticulous and regimented process. You can't just dig and strike gold. You can't plant it in a field and harvest it. You have to work for it. You need to understand the process and be faithful to it. Any shortcuts or missed steps will result in an inferior and polluted final product.

Even with all of our modern methods of producing gold, it still takes a lot of work and still takes a long time. We all know that there is fake gold out there. It can look shiny and legit from a distance, but after a closer inspection, you can see how fake it really is. As the old adage goes… "all that glitters is not gold." Gold worth having is gold worth paying for.

It's the same thing with our own process and journey. Sure, you could cheat the process with substance abuse and other addictions, but we all know that the relief is temporary and shallow.

As I began researching the process of refining gold, the parallels with refining our own lives and experiences were striking. The first thing to note is that gold doesn't grow on trees. You can't just find it all ready to go. That would be nice. However, that would also take away from its value. You have to start by mining for ore. Although ore can contain other minerals, our interest—for this example—is in the gold.

You begin by crushing the ore into smithereens. Heavy equipment and motorized machinery are used in modern times, but that was not always the case. You had to hammer and crush it by hand. It was an exhausting and lengthy process, but the payoff was worth the effort.

The more the ore was crushed, the finer the powder, the purer the gold. But we are getting ahead of ourselves. Before you can crush the ore, you have to extract the rock from the earth. It's not like you can take one truck filled with earth and have enough ore. No. In fact, big refineries will extract millions of tons of dirt to get enough ore.

Once you have crushed the rock sufficiently and are satisfied with the fineness, the next step is to thoroughly and constantly sift the powder. The sifting process is violent and vigilant, but is extremely important in the overall process. It prevents unnecessary pollutants from continuing in the process. Then it is further concentrated and purified. Then it's run through a very fine filter. It's squeezed and pressed as it goes through the filter. Intense pressure is then applied.

The final stage of gold production involves removing impurities that remain from the smelting process. Pure gold is generally too soft to be used on its own. Other metals are generally added to it so the gold can form an alloy. The melting point of gold is 1064° Celsius (1943° Fahrenheit). Gold has one of the highest melting points because of its resistance to heat.

Once it has melted into liquid form, it can be poured into whatever mold is desired—bricks or coins. It's interesting to note that useable gold is mixed with other metals in order to improve its strength. I'm sure by now that you are seeing the parallels.

Before we walk this out and start seeing the benefit of going through difficult experiences, it is interesting to note that even our dear friend Job understood and saw the connection between personal refining and the refining process of gold. He refers to it a couple of times. Here they are in the order that they appear:

But he knows the way that I take; when he has tried me, I shall come out as gold. —Job 23:10

"Surely there is a mine for silver
And a place where they refine gold.
"Iron is taken from the dust,
And copper is smelted from rock.
—Job 28:1-2

Well, after mining the ore, step one of refining gold doesn't appear to be the most encouraging or optimistic. The first step is to crush the rock into a fine powder, shake it relentlessly as you put it through the sifter. Then guess what happens next? You crush the rock some more, put it through the sifter again. You repeat this process until you are satisfied with the quality and fineness of the powder. I wonder how many of us have felt like that? I know I sure have. I know this step is necessary in converting cold, worthless rock into gold, but it seems a bit harsh, doesn't it?

How many times in your life have you felt that you were unfairly being beaten down by life? Maybe you blamed your parents, your spouse, your friends. Maybe you even blamed God. But what if everything you went through, you had to go through, in order to get you prepared for the next stage in the process.

I'm not saying that we should excuse the behavior that led to the crushing pain or disappointment in your life. I'm saying that it was a necessary step in the natural progression of your journey. Everyone wants the gold. Everyone wants to cross the finish line and claim the prize. I'm telling you, and I really wish that it was different, but you'll never see the pure gold until you are willing to endure the crushing.

The crushing prepares you for the filtering stage. Only that which is pure and good will be able to pass through to the next step. I know that we can feel caught and stuck within a vicious cycle of pain and progress. But I'm telling you, the two go hand in hand. The excessive pounding and sifting are what produce the best in us. It hurts. It's not easy, but it is necessary.

When we are in the midst of this process, it can often feel like it's never going to end. We can become disoriented and confused. It's difficult to tell up from down, wrong from right. It's like being enveloped by a gigantic wave in the ocean, it can cause us to lose our footing and get swept out to sea. But we have to hold on. We have to hold our collective breath, because I promise you, the waves will stop, the waters will calm, and you will be better for it. I know it's hard to believe, especially if you're in the middle of a crushing circumstance right now. But trust me…as someone who has gone through it, let me encourage you.

As difficult as this may be to accept right now and as counter-logical as it may sound, the crushing doesn't actually break you. You think that it will, but it doesn't. It literally makes you stronger. It's like looking at a bag of cement. What you see in that bag is the result of continuous and aggressive crushing. Yet, when that fine powder is mixed with just a bit of water, it becomes strong again. In fact, it doesn't just become as strong as it was in its original form, it can now be used to hold other things together as well. Isn't that encouraging? Isn't that a powerful illustration? When we submit ourselves to the process of crushing and sifting, not only do we come out stronger, but we can be the strength for others. For those who have yet to begin the process. It makes you stronger. It makes those around you stronger.

Phew. We made it through that stage! Time to relax, right? Time to take it easy and enjoy the gold, right? Wrong. As painful and as disorienting as the crushing stage was, the next step in the refining process can be brutal. It's brutal because, this is when the heat is applied. Yes, the crushing has removed a good amount of the impurities, but there are some things that can only come out with the heat. Ouch, right? As I look back on my own journey, my own process, I can remember the "heat". I can still remember the words and actions of people that hurt me more than I ever thought I could be hurt. The sting of betrayal. The bad taste of rejection. I thought it would never end. But you know what, it did. And it will end for you as well.

I wish that I could tell you there was an easier way to get gold. I wish I could snap my fingers and erase all the pain and heartache that you have ever endured, but I can't. Only the fire can do that. The more intense the pain, the more intense the fire needs to be. Fire and intense heat are the next step in the process of refining gold. I know this is difficult to accept, but deep in your heart, you know it's true.

Have you ever sat around a camp fire? It's one of the most relaxing things you can experience. There's something about watching the wood being consumed by the flames. The crackling of the fire, the warm glow of the charcoal. It's all just so peaceful.

An active campfire is a contradiction. Think about it. It's violent in the sense that the fire is eating through and destroying the wood. But the crackling sounds of this process are also as beautiful as they are peaceful. It's the same thing with us. Although enduring the fire can be difficult and painful, there is also something very cathartic about it.

Have you ever thrown a piece of paper into a fire? For a second, the paper just sits there, and for a moment, you think it may not catch fire. But it does. It always does. And so, you watch as that piece of paper transforms from whatever it was, into a small piece of ash. Even though the fire is intense and impartial, whatever was written on that paper is gone. And so it is with us. Although intolerable at times, we need the heat, we need the fire. It's what makes us stronger. It's what makes us pure.

Fire is the great equalizer. A $100 bill burns just as quickly as a $5 bill. Rich or poor. Black or white. Tall or short. The fire reduces all to ash.

Chapter 5—Worksheet

What do you find is your go-to reaction when something bad happens in your life?

Do you find it's a healthy or unhealthy reaction?

Have traumatic things happened to you that you feel you will never heal from?

Do you suffer from anxiety or panic attacks and if so, what triggers them for you?

How has your ash helped others? Or how have you used your ash to help others?

Chapter 6
THOU SHALL NOT COVET THY NEIGHBOR'S ASH

◇◇◇◇◇◇◇◇

I know that you can do all things,
and that no purpose of yours can be thwarted.
—Job 42:2

◇◇◇◇◇◇◇◇

I have to admit. Coming up with this chapter title has been my favorite so far. True, it is another clever play on words. And, like all those that came before, there is a much deeper meaning going on here. What does it mean to covet? And why in the world would you want someone else's ash?

Okay...let's start by defining what it means to covet: "to desire wrongfully, inordinately, or without due regard for the rights of others". And what does the ash represent in this scenario? It represents your past. Your pain. Your hurt. Your challenges. It represents all the things in your life that you struggled with and what you pushed yourself to do. In short, it's your journey.

When I tell you not to covet your neighbor's ash, this is what I mean: Don't look at someone who you consider to be successful, and assume they have it easy because they're famous or wealthy. You have no idea what they have been through in their life. You have no idea of what they have had to endure and how much they have had to fight to be where they are today. "Success" often comes at a price.

How many times have you heard about a new musical artist who takes the industry by storm? You have never heard their name before, and now, their songs are literally being played on every radio station you turn to. It seems like their success came overnight. I assure you, it did not. I have been fortunate in my life to become friends with certain individuals that many people would consider to be famous. I've been in their homes and they in mine. We have talked about many things over the years. And I can tell you, that they worked their butt off to get to where they are today. They were invisible for a long time. Most "overnight success" stories are years in the making, decades in some cases.

I've already talked about this, but I'm a huge soccer fan. Some of my favorite players come from the humblest of beginnings. They used to play in a dirt field that was full of bumps and stumps. If they were fortunate enough, they may have had some kind of old and hardly inflated soccer ball. Many of them had to be more resourceful. Today, they are some of the most well-known and highest-paid athletes in the world, but there was a time, not that long ago actually, when no one knew their name.

Today, I proudly wear their jersey as I travel around the world. So, don't covet someone's success unless you're prepared to take the same journey they did. They have ash. Lots and lots of it. The difference between some of us and them is…pause for dramatic effect…they got off their ash. They got comfortable with being uncomfortable. They were willing to put in the work that was necessary in order for someone to recognize that they had something to offer.

We have been looking at the life of Job and walking with him through one of the most tragic stories that has ever been recorded. Everyone loves the end of Job's story. That God restored to him twice what he lost. That the latter part of his life was greater than the first. People love the beginning and end of his story. But none of it would have happened without the middle. The pain. The suffering. The messy stuff. The stuff that no one wants to talk about. Everyone wants the dramatic Hollywood ending, where everything works out fine and the main character gets everything he ever wanted: love, money, and success. I can tell you from experience: no risk, no reward. No guts, no glory.

I have a journey too.

It's taken me many years to get to this place, and I won't lie, it feels really good. I can talk about myself and what I've accomplished without feeling embarrassed or sounding arrogant. They're just facts. These are the things that I have done. And I have done them because I got off my ash; because I dealt with the hurt and shame from my past; and I have learned to seek out discomfort. That's where dreams truly live. That's where real fulfillment dwells.

I got to a place in my life where I was willing to say "yes". Not a yes man, but yes to new opportunities.

Yes, to stepping outside of my comfort zone and walking into situations where I felt so intimidated and uncomfortable...I did it despite those feelings of inadequacy. And I always gave it my best.

I've stood on platforms with some "giants". We've shared the same speaking halls and ate at the same lunch tables at conferences and events. It didn't matter who I was on the bill with. What mattered was that I gave it my all and that I did my best. I always left everything out on the floor. I may not have been the biggest name, but I had a big message and I always gave it my best. Mediocrity is where dreams go to die. Passion and excellence are where dreams take flight.

I've had so many people over the years come up to me and say the nicest things about my messages and presentations. I also had some people who said things that were not so nice. It comes with the territory. I've had people tell me how blessed I am to have the opportunity to do what I do, and I am. But it wasn't like someone came to my house and offered me a book deal or a TV show while I was binge-watching stuff while sitting on my sofa at home. Guess what I did?

Yup, I had to get off my ash. I had to get over my feelings of deep insecurity and self-doubt. Some of you may find what I am about to say hard to believe, but it is 100% true. I used to be the shyest person you could ever meet. Yeah, me! I couldn't even go shopping for my own clothes as a teenager because I was too shy and scared to speak to the staff at the store. I have spoken to crowds of 15,000 people. I have preached at hundreds of churches in dozens of countries around the world, but it wasn't always this way.

I was told at a young age that I would never amount to anything. I carried that negative anchor of shame and doubt into my early 20's. I love speaking to a large crowd. It energizes me like nothing else. I love making people laugh. It's one of my favorite things in the world to do. No matter how bad of a day someone is having, when they laugh, even for a moment, they forget about whatever is troubling them. It's an incredible feeling.

I also love making people think. I love challenging people's preconceived ideas when it comes to certain Biblical passages. I enjoy walking someone from one side of an opinion to another. But it wasn't always that way for me. There was a time in my life where I faked being sick, on many occasions, just so I could skip the day in school where we had to get up in front of the class and give a speech.

I remember one time being forced to go to class. I gave my speech and was voted to present it to the entire school at the next assembly. I panicked. I don't remember what new illness I came up with to miss the event, but it worked because I never ended up having to do it. I still can't believe I did that. That's what fear can do. It controls you and can make you do things that you're not always proud of.

So, when people tell me that I'm a natural at public speaking or hosting a TV interview, it's really nice to hear, bu-u-ut it wasn't always a natural thing for me. As I stated previously, public speaking scared the life out of me. Just because someone makes something look easy, doesn't necessarily mean it is easy. It usually means that they have invested months or even years into becoming really good at what you are watching them do.

I really enjoyed attending Bible school because I loved the content. High school, not so much. But Bible school, I really thrived. That was until I learned that I would have to get up in front of the entire class and make a presentation. I'll never forget the first time I had to get up and speak in front of a large group in seminary. There were about 150 students or so in my class. I was so scared. I was so nervous and was dreading having to do it. I prepared my presentation and would rehearse it in front of the washroom mirror. I was comfortable with the material, but I had no idea how I would do when I actually had to stand up in front of the class.

I've said this before, and I'll say it again, I've always been and will always be proud of my Portuguese heritage. The one drawback, however, is my last name. I'm sure you've noticed that Amaral starts with "A". That means that I was one of the first students who would be called on to speak. There was only one student before me. Then it was my turn. Even as I'm writing this, I can recall the sinking feeling that I had in my stomach. I can still envision the seating arrangement of Classroom A. It was the typical lecture room setup. The first row is at ground level and the seats kept ascending as they reached all the way up to the back row.

The professor called my name. I walked up to the platform. We had to write our full names on the whiteboard. The other students were required to critique everything about our presentation. They were to judge us on the content. On the clarity with which it was being presented. They had to rate the volume and tone of our speaking voice. Our body language, posture, and even our hand gestures. I'll never forget how scared out of my mind I was as I started to write down my name. My heart was in my throat and my head was pounding from the anticipation and anxiety.

Then it was time to turn around. In my mind, I was going to face the audience, throw up, and leave in absolute shame and embarrassment. To my delight and complete surprise, I discovered that people actually enjoyed hearing me speak. I was shocked. Once I saw that people were genuinely interested in what I had to say, I began to feel more comfortable. The room broke out into spontaneous applause when I finished. If I'm being honest, it was a really weird feeling. Nice, but weird.

I didn't realize it at the time, but a shift was being put into motion. I would never go back to doing what I had done before that moment. Getting up in front of people was about to become the new normal thing in my life. And so it has been. The next time you watch me on YouTube or come hear me speak somewhere, and if you still think that I'm a natural, just remember, I had a lot of ash to deal with in my life. I'm still dealing with some of it, but for the most part, the big stuff is behind me.

Who I am today, in many ways, relates to Job. Obviously not to the same level of tragedy that he experienced, but the stage in life where I can look back on all the pain and negativity, and embrace it. We don't know how long it took Job to get off his ash. Here are the four verses I could find where Job makes a connection to the length of his suffering:

Job 7:3 says, "so I am allotted months of emptiness, and nights of misery are apportioned to me."

Job 29:2 says, "Oh, that I were as in the months of old, as in the days when God watched over me."

Job 30:16— "And now my soul is poured out within me; days of affliction have taken hold of me."

Job 30:27— "My inward parts are in turmoil and never still; days of affliction come to meet me."

It could have been days, weeks, or months. The point is that Job took whatever time he needed to grieve the loss, process it, accept it, then he was finally able to own his part to how he reacted and was able to go on with his life. In a very real way, Job was going through the various stages of grief. Everybody deals with them in a different way, but the truth is, we all go through them. Here are the generally accepted seven stages of grief:

- Shock, denial, disbelief and numbed feelings.
- Pain and guilt.
- Anger and bargaining.
- Depression.
- The upward turn.
- Reconstruction and working through.
- Acceptance and hope.

How you deal with them and how long you deal with them is totally up to you. Each person's journey is unique. There is no "quick fix" or magic pill. Sometimes I wish there was, but the harsh reality is that we often need to struggle and fight our way through until we achieve our goal or victory. The destination is worth the journey. The more we struggle the better and sweeter the victory will be. I'm sure you've heard it said before that anything worth having is worth fighting for. If that's the case, how much value would you place on your own personal freedom?

Getting off your ash will be one of the scariest things you ever do in your life. But I'm telling you, it's worth it. It's worth every tear. It's worth every challenge. It's worth it because you will become a new person. Just like the phoenix, you crash and burn, are reduced to a pile of ashes, and then you rise again. That's what I did, and that's what you can do too!

Fight. Fight for every step you take. You're worth it. It doesn't matter how long it takes. Every stage you go through will add something beneficial to your life. Think of your life and the process of getting off your ash as a complicated and delicate recipe. You may not always understand why certain ingredients need to be added, but the outcome would not be the same if you skipped a step. Everything you go through is another ingredient that will "flavor" the outcome of your life.

You and I may not have enjoyed every ingredient that has been added to the recipe of our lives, but I'm telling you, you would not be the person you are today without all of them. Although I struggled and suffered for many years, I'm happy with and proud of the person I am today.

Whether I like it or not or whether I want to admit it or not, the abuse I went through, the rejection I endured, the shame that I carried, ALL of it…I said ALL of it…has made me who I am today. And even though all that stuff caused me to go through some of the darkest seasons in my life, I wouldn't change a thing. Not a darn thing.

As I look back on the last five years of my life, I'm not sure I would have been able to do or accomplish half of what I did, had it not been for everything that happened to me over the course of my existence. I'm a better husband and father today. I'm a better teacher because of it. And I am a better missionary for the experience. I have a renewed empathy, passion, and compassion for the people I serve in Liberia. Despite everything and through it all, I am thankful for the whole kit-and-caboodle.

I didn't realize it at the time, but being told that I would never amount to anything became the subconscious fuel that drove much of what I have accomplished in my life. The sting of being sexually abused as a young boy had created within me a softness and a gentleness, that I don't know could have existed without that difficult experience. The wound of betrayal has cemented in my spirit the importance of family and friendship.

Next to being sexually abused, feeling betrayed has been the most painful experience I have ever had to endure. To know that your vulnerability was exploited is on par with the feeling of being violated. I know that sounds harsh, but in my case, it's the absolute God's honest truth.

So let me go back to the premise behind the title of this chapter. Again, just because someone makes something look easy, doesn't mean that it is easy. What it does mean is that they have understood and dealt with the pain in their ash. They made a decision to step away from their ash and to stop allowing it to have control over them. That they have taken their head out of their ash, meaning they no longer choose to dwell on the past and allow it to continue hurting them and chaining them down. It means they have gone through the fire. That they were forced to endure the painful process of being crushed almost to death. That they were exposed to the heat of the prolonged fire. It means that they have earned the right to do what they are doing. It means that they deserve to enjoy whatever success they amass in their field. Don't dismiss their journey.

I love it when people are affected by a presentation that I give. I love it when people are encouraged to step out of their comfort zone because of my story. That's what I want for every person reading this book. It's not about recklessly abandoning your career to chase down some childhood dream. No! It's about allowing yourself to become comfortable enough with saying yes to things that might be uncomfortable for you.

I could tell you about dozens of people that I have read about who got off their ash and sought out discomfort and ended up becoming legends in their own right. But this book isn't about them. It's about you, it's about me, and it's about our journey to becoming braver and bolder. It's about our quest to push ourselves beyond the borders of our preconceived comfort zones.

So let me tell you a little bit more about my journey. Let me tell you how I became comfortable with being uncomfortable. It's not about money, power or influence. It's about being honest about what really matters to you. I've had my share of these things in the past. But what I have today is far greater than anything I ever had before. Today, I have a sense of purpose. I know why I need to get out of bed in the morning. My social media isn't about me, it's about how I can use those platforms to benefit and help others.

My first book "Understanding Jesus" was published on April 7, 2011. It was a big milestone for me. No…it was a huge milestone in my life. I never dreamed that I, Joe Amaral, would ever have any company, never mind one of the largest publishers in the United States, want to publish anything I wrote. But they did. I remember traveling with my wife and children to New York City from Toronto in 2010 to sign the book contract. I didn't know what to expect. We walked into this beautiful building on the Avenue of the Americas. We were taken into this huge boardroom to go over the details of the contract. Once we were finished with that, they offered us a tour of their amazing office space. Out of nowhere, the legendary and talented Tina Fey walked by me. Other TV personalities were in the building, also there to sign a book deal.

I remember feeling like I needed to pinch myself. I never dreamed that anything like this could ever happen to me. To me, just another average Joe. I've never written about that experience before. In fact, I've only told a few people the details of that day. But I'm comfortable telling it now because I can honestly say that it's not about bragging or trying to be showy. I'm sharing it because I genuinely desire to inspire you to get off your ash and embrace the uncomfortable.

To this day, that was one of the happiest days of my life. That day was an accumulation of many years of trials and challenges. I didn't get an overnight book deal. It may have looked like that to some of you, but I promise you, it was not. There were many earlier drafts and versions of what eventually became "Understanding Jesus". There were lots of personal losses, financial setbacks and bogus book offers before this one.

My one regret is that my dad didn't live long enough to see it happen. He died less than two years before that first book deal. He and my mom came to Canada so I would have the chance for a better life. I did the next best thing. I dedicated that first book to my dad. You see, my dad got off his ash too. He did the most uncomfortable and bravest thing anyone could do. He left his country of birth. He left his friends and family behind. He spent his life savings to buy a one-way ticket to Toronto. He came to a country whose language he did not speak. He worked at a window factory for thirty years in order to provide for our family. He got up early and worked long hours. He got off his ash. He became comfortable with the uncomfortable. And then he died. You see, the loss of my dad, as painful as it was, turned out to be one of those necessary ingredients in the recipe of my life.

I love you, dad. I miss you every single day. Thank you for getting off your ash.

Chapter 6—Worksheet

Have you "coveted your neighbor's ash"—wishing you had their success or life?

____

____

Are there any fears that seem to control you and what you do?

____

____

If you're 100% honest with yourself, do you feel ready and willing to get off your ash?

____

____

What experience has most "flavored" your life's recipe and shaped who you are today?

____

____

Has there been that "subconscious fuel" that has driven you to either succeed or pull back?

____

____

Chapter 7
KISS YOUR ASH GOODBYE

◇◇◇◇◇◇◇◇

"Therefore I despise myself,
And repent in dust and ashes."
—Job 42:6

◇◇◇◇◇◇◇◇

Well, if you've made it this far, then you're probably pretty serious about getting off your ash. It means you're ready to make a change in your life. You're ready to get uncomfortable, and take back control of your life. Alternatively, you might just be one of those people who likes to read the ending first. Either way, we're going to take a good look at how to get off our ash…and stay off! It's not enough to simply get off your ash. It's a good start, but you can't just stop there. Your ash will keep trying to come back and knock you down. It will hit you when you least expect it. You'll be soaring high, doing great, and then…BAM!…it hits you out of left field, when you least expect it. That's been my experience.

This chapter is aptly entitled "Kiss Your Ash Goodbye". Again, not just another clever play on words. Although I have dealt with some pretty serious issues in this book so far, things like depression, anxiety, abuse and betrayal. This may be the most important section so far. You need to be able to die to the ash. What does that even mean? How do you die to the pain and shame of your past? What does a life that's dead-to-its-past look like?

Let me frame it this way: if your ash isn't dead, it will come back. I didn't say there was a chance it would come back. I said that it will come back. Anything that is not dead, no matter how weakened it is, given enough time, will come back to life. Your past is no exception. If you don't deal with the rejection from your past, guess what? You will continue to struggle with rejection in the future. Same goes for your self-esteem, your ability to trust again, and so on. You can't have a resurrection until a death occurs first.

We started this journey off by looking at the life of Job. Let's be honest, you never would have predicted how the end of his life would have turned out based on what you learned about him at the start of the book of Job. You have to give credit where credit is due. Although Job suffered and struggled for a long time, in the end, he got his act together.

Job didn't wish his feelings away. He didn't bury his head in the sand either, or pretend that his problems didn't exist. No. He faced them head on. Job says something so important in chapter 42:6, that I feel like an entire chapter could be written about it alone.

What does he say and why is it so potentially important in learning how to "Kiss Your Ash Goodbye"? What he shared may just be the most vulnerable statement I have ever read in my life, and I can surely identify with Job.

"Therefore I despise myself,
And repent in dust and ashes."
—Job 42:6

Not only does he admit to sitting in his ash, but he actually takes it one step farther. He literally says that he despises himself for it and that he is ashamed, and both regrets and repents of his behavior.

That's a huge statement to make. It's a massive thing to admit. To think it is one thing, but Job actually says it out loud where it has been preserved and recorded for all history, for all people, for all time, to see. Wow! Could you do that? That was the turning point in Job's life and in his recovery. He took a long time to get there, but he got there. We've mentioned the various stages of grief and how everybody goes through it differently. What's important is not how quickly you get through, but that you get through it in a healthy and safe way. Remember this line… "It's not about what happens to you, but what happens through you."

Job had to get to the end of himself. Job is the metaphorical boat tied to the dock that I referred to earlier in the book. He was a powerhouse who had the ability to change his world, but he wasn't going anywhere because he was still tied to the dock and was in danger of blowing his engine and suffering permanent damage. Job had to die to his ash. He could have spent the rest of his life looking at what had happened, but if he did that, he never would have received the restoration that was awaiting him. The past had to die, completely. It was the only way to ensure the coming resurrection.

Job had to get to the place in his life where he realized that what was happening to him, was even worse than what had happened to him. He had to arrive at the conclusion that his life's trajectory was heading for destruction. He had to despise what he was doing—not what was done to him. The difference is subtle on paper but is disproportionately different in the real world.

You see, it wasn't about despising the raiding invaders who destroyed everything he had ever worked for. It wasn't about despising the "Act of God" that killed his entire family. It was about despising his reaction to all of these events. It was despising the length of time he spent on his ash. There's a world of difference between the two. Would you agree?

I made the difficult decision to use my own life—the good, the bad and the ugly—as a comparison and an example to what getting off your ash can look like. There are lots of amazing stories out there of people who had to endure some pretty horrific things in their lives. Though my own story may pale in comparison to some of them, the bottom line is that it is my journey. I believe in transparency. I always have and I always will. Some people see transparency as a weakness. I disagree. In fact, I strongly disagree. I believe that transparency is the bedrock for building trust in any relationship. Even between author and reader.

Like Job, I too had to make a choice. Would I spend the rest of my life "licking my wounds" and living with the shackles of my past? Or, would I do the unthinkable? Would I get off my ash? I had to stop blaming my actions in the present on the actions of others in the past. I had to get to the place in my life where I was prepared to despise my actions. Are you prepared to despise your actions?

Job spent almost forty chapters defending his reaction and justifying his decision to sit on his ash. I think, if we're honest with ourselves, we'd all be a bit inclined to let Job sit there for a while. But, like Job, we need to make a decision. We need to decide whether we will spend the rest of our lives being governed by our past, or, make the tough decision get off our ash and leave it all in the past.

I had to make that choice too. Would I choose to be defined as a survivor of male childhood sexual abuse? Would I ever be ready to not only despise what was done to me, but to despise what I was doing and who I was becoming because of what had been done to me? How am I supposed to react to what happened to me? How do I rationalize it? How do I see the good in it? Was there good in it? These are some of the questions we wrestle with as we prepare to get off our ash. It's not easy, but it is necessary.

Do I despise the fact that as a young boy I was raped and molested by two fully grown men? Yes. Of course, I do. For a long time, I felt justified in taking the actions of the person I had become. Of course, I was becoming angry. I was raped and abused by men that I trusted, that were supposed to protect me, not take advantage of me. I allowed the memories of these experiences to justify the change in my character. I had no problem despising those men and what they did to me. But, and I hate to admit this, in the early days of all these awful memories resurfacing, I didn't have the strength to despise what I was becoming.

Like Job, we have to be ashamed of choosing to not just sit on our ash, but rolling around in it…using the painful experiences of our past to excuse the behavior of our present. We need to be ashamed. Not of what happened to us, but of what we have allowed to happen in us. It's important to understand and acknowledge what we went through. It's also important to understand that the bad things that happened to you are part of your journey, not your story.

Just like Job, it's decision time. We all want the second half of our lives to be better than the first, but are we willing to put in the necessary work? Are we willing to own our decisions and admit our mistakes? What about our shortcomings? Are we prepared to accept those also? Are we willing to confess that we have been sitting in a self-imposed prison made of ash and death? Read that again. It's absolutely ludicrous how we treat ourselves. We didn't commit the crime, but we voluntarily do the time. We blame, punish, and torture ourselves because of something that someone else did. In this case, to us.

The prison sentence ends today. It ends right now. Do you want to hear something crazy? We are the ones who keep ourselves imprisoned. We are the ones who play the role of judge, jury and executioner. Well, today is the day that you give yourself the gift of a pardon. Not only are you the only one who decides to stay in prison, you're also the one who decides to break the prison doors open and leave. Something beautiful happens when you choose to get off your ash. You start to see the world differently. You literally get a new vantage point. It's a whole new world.

So please do me a huge favor: get out and stay out! You may not have had the freedom or the ability to prevent what happened to you, but now, you're the one with all the power. Like Job, when you are willing to stand up and declare that you will no longer be shackled by the shame or hurt from your past, you can begin to experience freedom. The irony of freedom is that you have the right to remain in chains. So, that means that the opposite is also true, that you have the right to remain free. Free to live a life without regret. You have invested so much time and energy into sitting on your ash, into being held captive by your past. Now it is time to focus on the future. It's time to live.

It's time to be free and pursue what you are passionate about. It's time to start chasing the uncomfortable. Honestly, that's where joy lives. It may seem counterintuitive, but I'm telling you, it's the truth. But how do you know what you're passionate about? Here's a little trick that I have discovered from my own life: What would you be willing to earn less for? There's a very strong possibility that what you are willing to make less for, is what you are passionate about.

I spent most of my adult life trying to "make it". I bought the right clothes. I lived in the right neighborhoods. I even had the right jobs. I raised over ten million dollars for one organization that I was a part of for fourteen years. Because of it, I was invited to some of the biggest events in my area of influence. I was working so hard to cover up my old life that was caused by my ash, that I never stopped to ask myself if the life I was building was any better than what I had before.

I kept going from one great job to another. Seriously, by the world's standards, I was doing alright. In 2016, I was asked to join the staff as the main host of the longest running daily television show in Canadian history. The position came with what most people deem as being successful. It was a good paying job. My face was on basic cable across the country. I had the opportunity to speak into millions of homes every month. And, check this out, I even had a makeup person, hairdresser and wardrobe manager. Add to that, my fellow hosts and I really worked well together. We had great chemistry in front of the camera, and were honest-to-goodness friends.

Doing a daily live show comes with certain pressures. The news is always changing and guests were constantly either cancelling their interview appointments and others just happened to be in town. It was a lot of pressure. But honestly, I didn't mind. I think the busy-ness of everything helped distract my subconscious from focusing on my past. But I wasn't passionate about it. It was great, but deep down I knew this wasn't for me. It was easy, but it wasn't what I was passionate about. As I look back now and reflect on my time there, I only stayed as long as I did because it was kind of nice being the center of attention.

I enjoyed the custom designer suits. I enjoyed being recognized in public. I even ended up being next to Drake at a private balcony at a Toronto Blue Jays game. I can see now that all of it was part of an elaborate plan to cover up the pain that I was living with. I knew that one day people would find out about my abuse. And if I was popular enough, maybe, just maybe, people would overlook my past. It was a terrible reason to be in such a high-profile position, but yet, that's reason.

I left the TV show to join the staff of one of the largest churches in our fellowship. Same thing. I had the big office. We had three Sunday services that were getting more and more packed with each passing week. Our mid-week study grew from about fifty to four hundred in attendance in a matter of a few months. The position came with bragging rights. As far as my colleagues were concerned, I had it made. I had what a lot of other people wanted. Here's the thing though…I had everything except the one thing I needed most… passion!

I remember standing on the platform one particular Sunday. The place was packed. The cameras were rolling and the first of three services were live-streaming. Just like the ten-million-dollar organization, just like the TV show, things were going well, really well. But then I asked myself a question that I didn't even realize I was asking at the time. And it was this: Why are you here? Why are you doing this? The answer scared me. Because it was easy. What may have seemed scary, overwhelming, or even difficult for some people, came very easy for me. In that moment, I didn't know what was next, but I knew it wasn't where I was.

And so, I made a promise to myself. Whatever I would do next, no matter what it was, it needed to be something that I could not do without God.

It didn't matter if it was easy or difficult. It didn't matter what people would think or say. All that mattered was that I would be doing it for the right reasons. I was willing to take another high-profile position. I was willing to become uncomfortable in order to make others comfortable. I was willing to go to the ends of the earth if necessary. And wouldn't you know it…I did. I am now joyfully serving the people of Liberia in West Africa.

If I were to tell you the entire story of how I ended up serving in Liberia, I suppose it could be its own book. Who knows, maybe one day it will be. For now, let me give you the brief version. I travelled to Liberia with my son for the first time in April of 2019. Even before I left, my heart had already been broken for its people. On that first trip, we brought with us seven suitcases filled to the brim with toothpaste, toothbrushes, soap, medicines, crayons and other school supplies. It was awesome.

I travelled a bit before that first trip and tried to fund-raise as much as I could. We were not a registered charity at the time, so people were just giving out of the kindness of their hearts. We were able to raise enough funds to buy 150 backpacks, enough for every child in the school that we were going to visit. We were also able to purchase brand new uniforms and shoes for all the students. We visited villages that were way out in the jungle. The chief told us that we were the first people outside of the area to come visit them. We travelled across some pretty sketchy looking bridges. Some of the roads were barely passable at times.

I spoke of one of my village visits earlier. It was a life-changing experience to say the least. Since that first visit, I have been to several other villages. Then there are the children. The children always touch my heart. We always bring them clothing and rice when we go visit.

On one of my most recent trips to Liberia, during the COVID-19 global pandemic, we were able to purchase more than three tons of rice, and more than 1000 pieces of clothing. Once we were able to register a charity, things really started taking off. If you would like, you can see what we're doing by visiting our website at hopeforliberia.com.

At the time of this writing, we currently own five acres of land on the main road in a place called Careysburg. We renamed the area the "Community of Hope"—COH as it is known locally. We have a multipurpose building on the property. We have a school that can house more than 400 students with plans to complete a fully outfitted medical clinic in the near future. We have a school bus which transports children to school from the more rural areas. We also have a chicken coop on the land with more than 500 chickens providing approximately 15,000 eggs per month.

At the very beginning, we dug a well on the property and about 4000 people come each month to draw safe, clean drinking water. We are extremely grateful to our partners for helping us dig four wells so far in various counties around the country. We also brought electricity to the property. We provide job training at our trade school. And I hope that as you're reading this, we have been able to do so much more!

Liberia is hot. The economy is very fragile. Infrastructure is decades behind because of the back-to-back civil wars. Corruption is rampant. Liberia is one of the poorest countries in the world. At times, the needs can feel overwhelming. And did I mention, it is hot!?

And you know what?...I'm happier now than I have ever been in my entire life. No one knows who I am. No one cares about who I used to be in Canada. To them, I'm just Pastor Joe. Actually, they have given me a name from the Kpelle tribe: "Kolleh". It means, "man with bright skin". So basically, I'm known as Pastor White Guy. And I love it. And they love me.

When I first received the invitation to go to Liberia, there were zero dollars available for the budget. We had no money to buy the ticket in order to fly over. My friends and followers on social media provided the funds. We had no money to purchase supplies. The money came in. We had no money for the hotel. The money came in. As you can already see, a pattern began to emerge. Every time I stepped out of my comfort zone, boom, the provision started coming in to complete the projects we needed to do. I'd like to take full credit for all the fundraising, but I can't. Not even a bit. Remember what I said earlier?

Whatever I did next, it had to be something that I could not do without God. The land, the school, the bus, the chickens, the rice, the wells…all of it… it was all accomplished and provided for when I was willing to step out of my comfort zone and said YES. YES, to God. YES, to Liberia. YES, to the unknown. And most important of all: I said YES to getting off my ash.

Chapter 7—Worksheet

In your life, what ash needs to be completely dead—funeral and all—so that there can be a resurrection?

____

____

How have you been reacting to things that have happened to you in your past?

____

____

Are you prepared to "despise your actions"?

____

____

Is there good that you can see that has come out of the bad circumstances in your life?

____

____

What are you passionate about and what would you be willing to earn less money for in order to pursue that passion?

____

____

What do you want to say YES to?

Chapter 8
KICK YOUR ASH

◇◇◇◇◇◇◇

And the LORD restored the fortunes of Job,
when he had prayed for his friends.
And the LORD gave Job twice as
much as he had before.
—Job 42:10

◇◇◇◇◇◇◇

So, what was the point of this whole thing? Why write a book called "Get Off Your Ash"? The truth is, everybody has a bit of ash in their lives. I have to admit, this is the most fun I have ever had writing a book. Don't get me wrong, this has been hard work. I've sat at my desk for hours every day during the pandemic, writing and rewriting; reliving some pretty painful experiences. But it has been fun in that I have also been able to relive some pretty great things from my past. All of the ingredients of my life have helped make me who I am today.

It was also so much fun sharing the idea behind the book with some close friends and family members before its official release. Once I explained the premise of the book and how it was rooted in the story of Job, I always got the same two reactions. Most of the times, people would break out in heartfelt laughter. They all said the same thing. They believed that taking a humorous approach to a pretty dark topic, was the best way to go about it. Other people would cry as I began to explain about how the book speaks to the ash in our lives, the pain in our past.

Ash is all that remains after a violent death by fire. Fire is beautiful. Fire is deadly. In the end, the result is the same, no matter which walk of life you come from. If ash represents and is filled with death, then why do so many of us willingly choose to sit on our ash? Why do we keep going back to it? Why do we use it as a place of comfort? Our piles of ash are nothing but a collection of death. Think about that. They are all that remain from some of our darkest and most hurtful memories and experiences. Even though the ash is a vivid reminder of things that once were, in some cases, it's all we have left.

Think of all the things that you have not done in your life because you were held back by sitting on your ash. How many experiences, opportunities, friendships have you missed out on because of it. I want you to—I need you to—hear this: The things you don't do can have just as big of an impact on your life as much as the things you do do.

The time of missed opportunities ends now. Right here, right now, you need to choose. You need to decide that you will get off your ash. That you will surround yourself with people who will encourage you; people who will walk with you and do all they can to help you succeed. That they will rejoice when you rejoice. They will mourn when you mourn. Choose people who will celebrate your accomplishments and not be intimidated by them. Promise me that these are the types of people that you will choose to do life with.

Life is far too short to be carrying around a huge bag of ash. Some people carry their ash from relationship to relationship. You are poisoning and sabotaging yourself. There are people who will sense that insecurity in you and take advantage of it. I'm not pointing a finger at you. I've done this too. Like you, I've been hurt by people who were once close to me. I've had people turn against me because of my honesty and openness.

Even as I write this, I can feel the sting of some old wounds that run deep. Maybe you do too. Like me, you blame yourself and are trying to figure out what happened. Trying to think about what you did wrong. Here's the thing about betrayal—it doesn't usually come with an explanation. You might be sitting there, wondering what you did. The truth is you didn't do anything—that's what makes betrayal so difficult to get over. It seems to come out of nowhere.

Here's the truth, it says more about the other person than it does about you. Don't go through life trying to figure out what went wrong. Don't measure your value by the lack of value that others place on you.

I've said this before, I'm a visual learner. That doesn't mean that I can't learn by reading. It just means that I understand and make better connections when I can see it. Even if it is something just as simple as a word picture. Let me give you an example of what I mean:

0
00
000
0000
00000
000000
0000000

Have you ever felt like this? Like a zero? I sure have. Here's the thing. If you want to add value to your life, surround yourself with people who will champion your cause. Connect with people who will be your cheerleader, with people who will hold a light to your feet when its dark—not with people who place boulders in your path.

Let's build on the very simple "0" illustration that I just gave you. Even though we might feel like a zero sometimes, just watch what happens when we stand with the right ones:

10
100
1000
10000
100000
1000000
10000000

Look at how much value the right people can add to your life, to your self-worth and to your overall well-being. There are some people in this world who can add immeasurable value to your life. Make it your mandate to be that person for other people too!

Now, the opposite is also true. There are some people in this world who get some kind of sick pleasure from hurting people and holding them down. All that these types of people know how to do is to cause pain. All they do is bring ash into your life. They are a never ending, bottomless pit and supply of ash. It's almost as if they are like wells. Instead of providing water, they produce ash—hurt, pain and feelings of rejection. Here's the thing about a well, no matter how deep you go, no matter how much water you draw, there's always more.

These water holes are an endless source of life-giving water and there will be people in your life who will be like that to you…they will be your water-holes. But…at the opposite end, there are also those people who are like other holes; conversely, these holes produce ash. If a water well can be known as a water hole, then I suppose those people who are a never-ending supply of ash could be called…ash-holes. These bottomless pits can be people, and they can also be companies or organizations. You need to distance yourself from that kind of negativity. Stay away from those who produce ash in your life.

Think of it this way. Imagine if you were standing next to a person that was wielding a knife in your general direction. Let's say that the motion was directed towards your back. As I see it, you have one of two choices. Remain where you are and keep getting stabbed in the back relentlessly and endlessly. Or…move.

Have you ever been watching a movie where the main character is running away from a fast-approaching object that looks like it's about to run them over? And you're wondering to yourself… don't try to outrun it…just get out of the way of its trajectory!

I think the answer is obvious to most of us. You would move, right? It's the same way with these bottomless pits of hurt—these ash holes—you need to walk away from them. I'm not suggesting you pray for the plagues of Egypt to fall on their lives; we're not hoping for anything bad to happen to them, but you need to put some space between you and them. You need to get out of the splash zone… perhaps even the slash zone. You need to make a decision in your life that you will no longer give these bottomless pits of pain and hurt the right to hurt or hinder you. Do it now. Revoke their right to enter your space and fill the air with toxic thoughts and negative energy.

I know that this is easier to say than it is to do. What if they have been life-long friends? What if they are people that you have been working with for a very long time? All I can do is speak from my experience. Personally, I would rather be alone with one or two true friends than in a room full of bottomless pits of hurt and death: ash holes. But hey, that's just me. Putting distance between you and them will grant you the opportunity to catch your breath. It will allow you to experience what toxic-free air feels like. Choose distance over disrespect.

It's not about getting back at people who constantly hurt you. It's more about a refusal to allow them in your space where they can hurt you. It's about getting away from things like the passive-aggressive comments whenever you share successes; the veiled and backhanded compliments.

Your need to be accepted should never outweigh your duty to remain authentic.

When you get off your ash, it provides you with a deeper and more confident opinion of who you are and the value you hold. Say no to those bottomless pits of pain. I mean literally, right now. Put the book down and imagine the person or persons who have endlessly and relentlessly caused you hurt and pain: the ash holes in your life. I want you to look at them, put up your hand, and say NO.

NO, you will not allow them to continue poisoning the air you breathe. NO, you will no longer let them put toxic thoughts in your mind about yourself. NO, you will no longer falsely justify that the length of time you have known them will make it difficult to put distance between yourself and them. It's not the length of the relationship that matters, it's the depth. Those shallow, toxic, poisonous relationships stop now. You matter way too much to be held down and held back by these bottomless pits of ash, these ash holes.

I really wish I could give you "three simple steps" to getting off your ash. I'd love to tell you that I discovered a secret formula so that you would never have a negative thought again, but I haven't.

The truth is that what worked for me may not necessarily be the thing that works for you. We all discover and process information in different ways. So, there really is no universal method of dealing with trauma, disappointment, betrayal, abuse or abandonment, or any other circumstance you find yourself in.

One thing that worked for me, and I would encourage you to do, is something that I learned from my counsellor. She told me to write a letter to the people who had hurt me, to the people who had betrayed my trust and my innocence. She told me to write the letter as if I was going to send it to them. She told me not to hold back; to say whatever it was that I needed to say, in whatever way I needed to say it. To not censor myself, but to just let it pour out of me. And after the letter was written, I was free to do whatever I wanted to do with it. I could send it to them. I could burn the paper. I could delete the file. What mattered in the process was that I would get the poison out of my system.

And so, I did it. I sat down at my computer and started to type. It was awkward at first. I had never done anything like that before, so the words weren't coming out naturally—not at first, at least. But the more I began to write, the more the words began to flow. I began to relive emotions that I had buried for a long time.

There was no shame in the letter, neither was there any guilt. Instead, anger began to bubble up inside of me. Normally, I was mad at myself and I would blame myself for what happened to me as a child, but not this time. I was mad at them. I was incredibly angry at what they did to me. I didn't expect it to feel as good as it did, but letting it out was one of the most cathartic experiences I've ever had in my life.

For the first time ever, I was able to even consider forgiving what these monsters had done to me. You see, forgiveness doesn't excuse the other person's behavior. Forgiveness releases you. It simply releases you from carrying the pain of what they did. There's a very powerful quote from Marianne Williamson that speaks to this very thing: "Unforgiveness is like drinking poison yourself and waiting for the other person to die." Similarly, Nelson Mandela said, "Not forgiving someone is like drinking poison and expecting the other person to die."

Remember though, you still get to control and limit how much exposure you have to the person or people who hurt you. Forgiving doesn't necessarily mean that things go back to the way they were. Sometimes they can, but in most cases, they don't. And that's okay. You're not responsible for what they did to you, but you are responsible for how you react to it now and for how long you hold onto it.

So, write that letter. Record a voice memo on your phone. However you choose to do it, it's important to get all those toxic and negative feelings and emotions out of your body and mind.

Another thing I would say is to listen to your body. Our subconscious mind is far more powerful than we will ever be able to understand. For years before I finally started to remember what happened to me, my body was trying to tell me, but I wasn't ready to listen. Have you noticed a steady and increasingly noticeable level of anxiety in your life? Maybe you've been suffering from insomnia and it has been getting worse with time. Have you noticed that it's been getting easier to fall into depression and that it's lasting longer and longer? Whatever it is that you have been experiencing in your physical body, it's possible that your mind is trying to tell you something. You should listen. It nearly killed me.

I would also encourage you to tell someone. These aren't things that you post on social media, and they are not things that you share with everyone you meet, but there must be at least one person that you trust enough to tell these intimate things to.

I know it's scary. Maybe you feel the same way I felt before I told my wife about everything that happened to me. Maybe you thought that people would start looking at you differently or think less of you. And you know what, there might be some who do those things. But the people who know you—I mean who really know you—you just might be surprised by their reaction. Secrets breed in darkness. When you expose the lies you're believing to the light, they scatter like cockroaches. Find that person; tell your story; find your peace.

Your life can start changing now! Some people like to use the eagle as an illustration for power and prosperity—that you should rise with wings of eagles and soar high above all of life's problems. Not me. I would suggest that life and prosperity is more like that of the phoenix. You rise. You fly. You crash and burn. You rise again. It doesn't matter how many times you crash; the key is to rise and fly again. This journey began with Job, and so I feel it appropriate that we end our time together with this example of the phoenix from the life of Job.

It's important to acknowledge and identify the pain in the ash. As you work through that pain, the next step is to move your ash. The process of putting distance between where and how our ash has held us back is an important one. Once we leave it, we have to stop going back. That's why it is important to take your head out of your ash. We have to leave our ash behind. We have to learn that the hot ash in our past—though difficult to endure—is what melts away the impurity and eventually makes us stronger than before or than we could ever imagine. We have to stop coveting our neighbor's ash. We do this by recognizing that everyone has a big old pile of ash in their past. That no matter where we are, we are all on a journey. Always remember how valuable you are. No situation that continually and constantly adds ash to your pile is worth it. You need to kiss your ash goodbye and keep on moving forward. Get rid of everything toxic in your life. It's time to kick your ash to the proverbial curb.

So, dare to dream a little more. Force yourself to leave your place of comfort once in a while. It's not necessarily about leaving what you have for something new. It's about allowing yourself to reach that place of personal healing in your life, where you are not afraid to live in the uncomfortable for a minute.

That's it. That's all I have to say. I may not know who you are or how this manuscript got into your hands, but with all the love I have in my heart, let me say this to you…

Get off your ash!

Chapter 8—Worksheet

What things have you not done because you were held back by sitting on your ash?

____

____

Of your friends and family, who encourages you and rejoices with you in your accomplishments?

____

____

Who, in turn, do you encourage and cheer on in their successes?

____

____

Is there anyone in your life you can think of who could use that encouragement? If so, who?

____

____

What ash hole or pit do you need to step back from or distance yourself from in order to move forward?

____

____

Who, in your life, do you trust enough that you would be comfortable sharing the details of your past with?

____

____

Think about what you would write and how you would want to say it. Then take a sheet of paper (or two or three maybe) to write the letter(s) to the person(s) who have contributed to the ash in your life.

Honorable Mentions

Here is a list of chapter titles that didn't make the cut:

Ashes to Ashes
Nice Ash
Work Your Ash Off
Stop Dragging Your Ash
Laugh Your Ash Off
Bad Ash
Sorry, My Ash
Kiss My Ash

Acknowledgements

◇◇◇◇◇◇◇

This is the part in the book where I finally get the opportunity to shine a light on others. It's here that I acknowledge how absolutely useless I would be if I tried to do this alone. Thankfully, I've never had to worry about that. I have been extremely blessed to have the people in my life that I do.

While this is, by no means, an exhaustive list, it is an acknowledgement of people who helped make this book project possible. They are some of the people who helped me turn this crazy idea I had into a book that I can say that I am very proud of. I can only hope and pray that it will find its way into the hands of those who need it most.

My wife Karen has always been my number one fan and my greatest supporter. She has walked beside me through this entire journey. She encouraged me when I was at my lowest points in life. She believed in me even when I didn't. I know that I would have not had the strength to get off my ash on my own. She was with me every step of the way. In the darkness, she was my light. She was my compass when I felt lost. She saw me through the worst, and has helped me become my best. I love you, Karen Amaral.

I'd also like to acknowledge the tremendous contribution made by my friend, Todd Stahl. I knew this was the book I wanted to write. I knew I had it in me, but I just couldn't find the proper phrasing for the title. It was Todd who got me there. It was Todd who made the connection between what I wanted to say and the story of Job. He showed me a card that he had drawn a few years before where he actually used the phrase "Get off your ash" and quoted Job 2:8. The moment he said it, everything clicked, and the book flood gates were blown wide open. Not only was Todd crucial in coming up with the title for this work, he's the talented artist behind the ash pile on the cover of this book! Thank you, Todd for gifting me with this brilliant phrase and amazing artwork. I did it, buddy. I got off my ash.

I'd also like to acknowledge everyone who has in one way or another contributed to who and what I am today—all the good, the bad and the ugly that I've been through. I'm thankful for the sweet, and I'm thankful for the sour. I'm thankful for the delicious, and I'm thankful for the unappetizing. I didn't know it at the time, but all of them were a necessary ingredient in the recipe that is my life.

To the people of Liberia. It is an absolute honor to love and serve you. You will never fully know how much you saved me. You might think that it is I who is helping you, but the truth is that you have helped me more than you will ever know. You have given me purpose. You have brought me unimaginable joy. From your children to your elders, I love you. I can't wait to see what happens next.

Other Works by Joe Amaral

Understanding Jesus

What Would Jesus Read?

Story In The Stars